Abiding Sorrow

A Daughter's Account of Loss and Grief

By Pam Robbins

Lulu.com

Robbins, Pam

Abiding Sorrow

A Daughter's Account of Loss and Grief

ISBN 978-0-557-36136-6

Published by Lulu.com

Printed and bound in the United States of America

Table of Contents

Acknowledgements

Thanks to Annie Emanuelli for providing endless help and support; Ellie Cook and Bill Lewis for policing the grammar; and Gloria Girouard, Greg and Sheilah Sandler, Christie Wilson Krusz, Sandy Milenski, and Sally Boutiette for encouraging this project.

For Lucia: everything, always,
and for my friends.

Introduction

This project began as a series of reminiscences—and lamentations—spoken into a small recorder and stored on mini-cassettes on an almost-daily basis for nearly a year. The thoughts expressed, totaling hundreds of pages, later were transcribed and then edited into a journal that is at the heart of this book.

These pages are deeply personal and frankly sentimental. They tell of a mother-daughter relationship—and a friendship, forged by hard times; severed, but not broken, by death. The intent of this effort was twofold: to provide a means for me to give voice to my heartbreak and thereby to survive it; and to speak a word of empathy to others who have lost the person whom they loved most. This little book stands as proof that somehow we go on.

Chapter One: Arm in Arm

When I have not thought about my mother in a little while, and someone or something brings her to my mind, I see her first as she was 40 years ago, walking down our street, wearing a checked coat, grasping a grocery bag or two.

I stand in the living room window and watch, and when she is close enough for me to see her face, I bolt from the house and run to meet her. She smiles in greeting and my heart swells. I may take a bag from her or she may refuse my help, in either case I tuck my hand in the crook of her elbow and we walk the rest of the way together.

That image holds me fast because it represents the essence of our relationship: We two, together, struggling and overcoming, the odds and the obstacles life can present for a mother abandoned by her husband and raising her only child alone.

There are others.

Our house sits on a curve so that when I begin the half-mile trek from the corner, I already can see the light in the window. Beyond that light, I know, she is working in the kitchen, or, in later years, waiting in her big armchair for the sound of my step on the front porch. She smiles in greeting and my hearts swells. Still, always, there is that instant of delight in seeing this woman who has been my parent, my dear friend, my companion in life.

I see her sturdy frame bent over a shovel or rake in the yard. Her lot was not to tend blooming flowers or burgeoning vegetables in some garden. She was the one who mowed and raked and hauled big bags of brightly colored leaves to the curbside. I see myself beside her, holding the bags open in the early days, then working side by side with her. Much later the task become mine, then was passed to a hired man. Still, she would check her yard, clip a branch here, pick up a stray paper there. I would slip a palm under her forearm to give her balance.

And so the years passed for us: Christmases with trees that became smaller each year, and then disappeared, leaving it to the red velvet angels to herald the season; birthdays with cakes that also dwindled in size, and cards whose sentiments grew more expansive.

We did not plan it that way—that I should grow middle aged alongside her as she grew old. But that is how it turned out.

We had thought that I would have a life quite apart from hers, a life filled with triumphs she could share. There have been a few. If there have been as many heartbreaks, it did not matter much; they were shared by her as well.

We had thought that she would visit me in another house, another town, another world. Instead, I have remained a bedroom door away. I have no regrets. No one ever has made me laugh more, given me more wisdom, more joy.

Sometimes on a winter night, we sit together, reading or watching a movie and I look up to see her engrossed in the story, or dozing quietly and I think, "This is enough." Sometimes in the early morning, just after midnight, I wake at night and peek in on her, just to be sure she is still breathing, completing that circle of concern begun when I was born.

"Two hearts that beat as one," we say. "Cut one, the other will bleed."

"It is enough," I tell myself over and over.

The pain is in knowing it is not forever.

I like to think there is an afterlife, though I lack certainty and the comfort it would bring. Still, I think, so much love, so much energy must go somewhere. I like the stories people tell of passing through tunnels into white light and meeting loved ones on "The other side." I think that whichever one of use goes last, my mother or myself, will be met by the one who went first.

We will smile in greeting and both our hearts will swell.

And we will walk the rest of the way together.

***

The above piece was written in

September 2000, for the Daily Hampshire Gazette in Northampton, Mass. Ironically, it was not printed until Nov. 24, 2000, the day after my mother died. Later, it appeared in "Chicken Soup for the Mother and Daughter Soul." It is a summation of sorts, but it does not begin to tell her story or ours.

***

My mother's death was the end of my own life as I had known it.

I am a woman who in some ways was never a child. Abandoned by my father when I was 5, molested by my stepfather for several years, I understood early on that life is hard and people are seldom what they seem.

I am also in some ways a child who has been unable to recover from the loss of her mother. I was 55 when she died. There was a small gap between her aging process and my own, and often I feel unequal to the tasks and losses that lie ahead.

I was in my 20s when I first began to struggle with the notion of a God who knows us by name and cares about us. Longing to believe, I have spent large chunks of time since then grappling with doubt and cynicism, occasionally grabbing hold of something that passes for faith but never fully at peace with it. To date, no epiphany has come to save my sanity or my soul.

The only certain thing; the only anchor was Lucy, my dear mother, my companion in life. Since her death nine years ago, I have been lost, afflicted by a ceaseless knot in my gut, an unrelenting anxiety. What will I do? How will I manage old age, failing health? How will I do all of it all alone?

I seek answers as I always have—in the written word. If I write it, I can control it. I can make it make sense. I don't know what the future holds for me but I know what the past held and where it has led me. This is that story.

Chapter Two: The Fall

We had shared a piece of apple pie that June evening in 1994, and then I left the restaurant first, to bring the car around so she wouldn't have to walk so far. I should have made her sit inside until I came back for her. Instead, I told her to wait until she saw me pull up and she did. She smiled at me and started down the brick path to the town sidewalk.

I smiled back and then I saw her smile turn to fear as she missed the single concrete step to the walk. She toppled like a tree; her temple met the pavement first.

I heard myself say, "Oh my God" over and over and it occurred to me I should stop saying it, but I couldn't. She was unconscious for a minute. Her eyeglasses were broken. There was blood on her face and under her head.

The food server I had just tipped came out to help. "Don't worry," she said with the confidence only a 20-year-old can muster. "I'm trained in first aid." She kneeled down and began to comfort my mother. I ran inside to the pay phone and tried to get ahold of my best friend, Annie. I had no cell phone then.

The ambulance was there in minutes. Mom kept trying to get up. The EMTs kept dissuading her. They put her on a gurney, sitting up. She was having trouble breathing. We learned later that she had broken a rib and the rib had pierced the lung. She had a pneumothorax.

As they got her ready to transport, someone from the restaurant parked my car for me. I climbed into the cab of the ambulance to ride with the driver. I was crying and my heart was pounding. I held her pocketbook against my chest. The driver tried to distract me with small talk, but I could hear my mother in the back saying to the crew, "Are you mad at me?"

Minutes later, we pulled into the hospital's emergency lot and backed up to the platform. I rushed inside. My hands were shaking so much I could hardly pull out her insurance cards. When the paperwork was done, I made some calls.

A nurse said I could go into the treatment area. By then my mother had begun to make less sense as her head injury caused the brain to swell. They were concerned about her breathing. "Your mother's lungs are very bad," the ER doc told me in a chiding tone, as though I had withheld that information. I had no choice but to let them intubate her. "She'll be terrified," I told him. "She'll be asleep," he said.

Someone told me that Annie was outside in the hall. During that first frantic hour, other friends also arrived. I called Mom's physician and he promised to contact the hospital—where, unfortunately for us, he was not on staff—to urge the doctors not to give up on her. (Over the next weeks and months, he and I fought shoulder to shoulder for her.)

The nurse told me the ER doctor wanted to talk to me and she ushered me into a small room. That's when I panicked. If it's good news, they tell you where you're standing.

I remember listening to the doctor's assessment and then asking, "Are you saying that this could be life-threatening?" I don't remember his words. But I remember the gist of his answer: Yes.

"We were eating pie an hour ago," I said. He did not respond.

Friends drove my car home. I waited. When they brought my mother up to the intensive care unit, Annie and I followed the gurney and made a place for ourselves in the waiting room. Over the next nine days, a stream of visitors came and went—mostly people from the newspaper where I worked. I had made the decision not to tell my mother's family that she had been injured. She would not know if they came; and they would only irritate me.

The nurses in the ICU were wonderful. I was surprised to find that one of the best had come from pediatrics when there was a cutback in staffing. She still had a teddy bear on her badge.

As for the doctors, I had barely sat down in the waiting room when the internist and the pulmonologist told me I should think about discontinuing life support. The chubby internist kept saying, "Sorry" after every dire pronouncement. He drew it out into two syllables, "Sor – ry." The pulmonologist wore what appeared to be the same pair of maroon polyester pants for several days. They had a stain on one leg that looked like semen or snot. I despised both men for writing my mother off too soon. I opted for hope.

On the ninth day, it was clear to me that Mom was strong enough for us to transfer her to Baystate Medical Center, the region's tertiary-care facility, for which I had done freelance work for nearly two decades and for which Annie was then director of publications. I had asked about moving Mom when she was first injured but she was not then stable enough. Now she was.

The internist immediately threw up a wall of *can't.* "They won't do any more for her there. They won't take her." We kept hammering at him until he agreed to call. When he returned, he fairly shouted, "They took her." Within 30 minutes, she was loaded onto an ambulance, an R.N. by her side, for the ride down Interstate Route 91 to Baystate.

We went in Annie's car and were watching when they wheeled my mother past the ICU waiting room to the unit. The minute I saw her ensconced in the pod, I felt relief surge through me. She looked safe and comfortable. Someone had put glycerin on her chapped lips. There were three docs in green scrubs at her bedside: an intensivist, a pulmonologist, and an emergency medicine physician. They did not look hopeless or helpless. They looked engaged and determined. If she dies now, I said, I'll know I did everything I could.

Chapter Three: The Struggle

She endured 47 days in acute care and another 20-something in a rehabilitation facility, a place I hated in the extreme. Finally, she returned home after Labor Day. But it was not a happy ending. It was a stop along the way on a journey that ultimately left our peace and happiness behind. The hospitalizations had just begun and would become a recurring pattern.

I remember one event especially because I recounted it in a journal I kept sporadically over the next six years. At 2 o'clock one winter morning, she was sitting on the edge of her bed. She wanted to go downstairs. I asked if she could wait until 4 a.m. I needed a little more sleep.

She said that would be OK and I went to my room. The baby monitor was on. I would hear her if she needed me.

But I didn't.

When I woke at 4 and went in to get her, she was sprawled sideways on the bed. Her arms were thrown over her head, her chest thrust forward. She was soaked with sweat. Her oxygen cannula was lying beside her. "Help me," she gasped over and over.

I managed to prop her into a semi-sitting position and begged her to let me put the oxygen back on her. She didn't understand what I wanted. I doubt she even knew who I was.

I was frantic. With no phone in her room, I had to leave her to call for help, and hope she'd last till I got back.

I called from my room, pulling on my clothes as I talked to the dispatcher, who instructed me to open the doors. I did. Emergency medical personnel soon crowded the room with its low ceiling. "Do you have a do-not-resuscitate on her?" one asked. My heart lurched. "No." I said. They began working.

Two police officers were on the scene as well. They told me to go ahead to Baystate and start a chart on her. As I drove to the hospital, I kept saying, "Please God." I thought the ambulance was right behind me. It wasn't. I think they had trouble getting her stable enough to transport. I was afraid she would be dead on arrival.

Between calling the ambulance and opening the doors for the crew, I had called Annie. It was about 4:30 in the morning and bitterly cold, but I needed someone and I knew she would come. "I'll be there in 20 minutes," she said. That was impossible, I thought. But she made it in 25.

I remember her face, red from the cold, anxious beneath a big purple woolen hat. She hurried through the automatic doors, talking to me even before she reached me. She stayed with me that day, a Friday, the following Saturday and Sunday and beyond, until my mother left intensive care.

Somehow during the days and nights at Mom's bedside and in and out of chilled cars and overheated buildings, Annie lost that purple hat. I kept hoping it would turn up. But it never did. I still feel inordinately sad about that. I will remember that hat as long as I remember her rushing through the door and staying with me throughout that long desperate time.

That morning we waited in the ER cubicle as my mother lay on a gurney, intubated and pale, dozing quietly as doctors tried to figure out how to help her.

There was a nurse in scrubs nearby. She was very petite, so much so that her head and big hair seemed to overpower her body. Annie dubbed her the "giant-headed midget nurse," and we began to laugh, almost hysterically. I said, "She looks like a character in ER on Parade." Annie reached up and gripped her own head as though trying to remove it, and whined, "Do I have to wear the head againnnn?"

We knew even then that we were being dreadfully inappropriate, but our laughter was about finding a spark of life in an atmosphere thick with death, and surviving an ordeal that was to mutate, ebb and flow, but not really relent for years.

Again my mother rallied. She came home. Again we adjusted, adapted, altered schedules and surroundings. It became the story of our lives.

***

At some point I began sleeping on the living-room couch and my mother began sleeping in an overstuffed chair. We were about 3 feet apart. When she woke, I woke.

I could not sleep upstairs and leave her alone downstairs. Not with a 50-foot oxygen cord around her neck. Not when she might awaken confused or off balance.

So we called it camping out.

Every night as we watched TV I would put a sheet on the couch, slip cases over the pillows and lie down. She looked so small, swathed in throws and blankets. Sometimes she wore what she called her "gold" woolen hat, which was actually brown. It was at least 70 degrees inside but she was cold.

She talked in her sleep and I teased her about it. "Maybe I'm not really sleeping," she joked back.

When the alarm went off at 4:45 each day, I would look to see that she was breathing. If she was, it was a good day.

"You'll be taking her home soon," I whispered to a god I did not wholly believe in. But even when she and I used to talk about what I would do when she was gone, neither of us believed she would go. How could she be anywhere I could not reach her? It was from our relationship that I took my sustenance, my reason for being.

It was as if the cord had never been cut, but it was more than that, because, in our case, the dependency was mutual: She took her strength from me as well. I told the same elusive god: "Just let me be what she needs." That passed for prayer in my life.

***

I worried even more after she had gastrointestinal bleeding one Tuesday in August. I came downstairs and she told me to sit down. She asked me to tell her again about the time in the hospital when she had begun bleeding and crashed. It was an episode she did not recall, except as I had first recounted it to her.

Unsure why she was asking, I told her again how one minute she had been sitting in her hospital bed talking to me, and the next there were several doctors gathered around her and a nurse literally running back and forth – I think to get meds. They pushed me out of the room, but somehow Annie ended up standing beside the bed a few minutes longer. My mother squeezed her hand and told her, "Don't be scared."

Outside the door, one of the doctors told me, "She's still with us—but just barely. We're taking her back to the unit (the ICU)."

They didn't expect her to survive. But she did. That happened twice more—her being rushed from a room to the intensive care unit because of GI bleeding. The prognosis was not good. At one point, Annie and I stood beside her. I focused all my love and hope, and Annie, a Reiki practitioner, did what she could. The bleeding stopped. We will never know why—not for sure.

The doctors blamed the bleeds on C-difficile, a kind of colitis caused by antibiotics, so I became a watchdog over her medications. "She needs very specific antibiotics," I would tell anyone who would listen over the next several illnesses. "You need to be careful." Sometimes they seemed to pay attention. Other times they acted as if I were nuts.

On this August afternoon, in our home, she listened to the story of that episode, and then told me she had been bleeding again. She spoke calmly—for my sake, I'm sure.

I took her to the ER and we were there five hours. The good news was that she came home the same night. She was scared. "I'd like to be around a little while longer," she said in a small voice, trying to smile. That crisis resolved itself and life went on.

Chapter Four: Our Yard

As her health continued to deteriorate, my mother lost the ability to work outdoors. It was one of her bigger losses. She loved to rake and prune.

I remember that we were both so happy when we bought a sliver of land, part of an overgrown parcel behind our house. The extra land pushed back our fence line and kept the teenagers from congregating right outside our back door. We felt like landed gentry.

I pitched in and together we cleared that piece, or tried to. We spent days at it. Then we noticed that someone was bulldozing a parcel nearby.

I walked over, picking my way across the ruts left by the 'dozer, slipping in the soft, moist dirt. I pitched the idea to the guy: Turn our little plot for 50 dollars. He sat there, smug, looking down at me. Then he nodded.

I made my way back. Then Mom and I waited anxiously, afraid he would rethink it. But he came, turned the dirt, took the cash, and rode away. Our hero. My mother looked out at the level ground, minus the stumps and clumps and rocks that had marred it. Delighted, she literally clapped her hands, and then grabbed her rake. My heroine.

The yard had mostly crab grass, but also lots of shrubbery around the perimeter and a few pine trees she had planted as scrubs, grown to 20, 30, even 50 feet tall. There was a maple tree as well. A former friend had brought it home from a walk, having yanked it up by its roots in a vacant lot up the street. It looked like little more than a branch. My mother stuck it into the ground. It flourished.

"You should leave here when your mother goes," everyone used to tell me. "Too much house; too much work, and the neighborhood isn't safe."

I would look at those trees and picture her digging the holes, filling them in, dragging the hose over. Everything was always so goddamned hard for her. But she was always so determined; undaunted, asking so little from life, getting even less.

The trees took root and grew. To me they were a testament to her will, and to the power of her nurturing. How could I leave those trees behind?

Chapter Five: Life and Loss

We always argued a lot, and as she aged it seemed we fought more often. She would get upset and so would I and we would wind up screaming at each other. I knew it was the worst thing for her; I felt the physical strain of it as well. But you had two volatile Italian women, both weary and frustrated and fearful of a separation that was looming.

So we shouted and swore and clutched our respective chests. Ten minutes later, we were drinking tea and laughing about why we "could never live in a condo," where the neighbors would hear us.

As time passed, she grew frailer, until she became dependent on me for all the things she used to do. My life during the last years of hers was not what I had in mind. The drudgery, anxiety and despair, fear and anger—they were not what I wanted or dreamed of or hoped for. But they were what I got, and what she got in turn.

I was not as good as people thought, or as good as she deserved, or as good as I wanted to be. I yelled—about anything and everything. I snapped and sniped and whined. I griped if she talked to me and I couldn't hear her, and if I talked to her and she couldn't hear me; if she dropped used Kleenex; or didn't make room for her teacup on her TV tray; if she didn't remember a movie we had seen the previous month.

Sometimes she fought back. Sometimes she didn't bother. She said once, "You think I'm the mommy you used to have. But I'm not that mommy anymore." Always she tied a knot in my heart. One night she was asleep in her chair. She opened her eyes suddenly and waved a hand gently to say hello. She smiled her impossibly sweet toothless smile.

"You'll be all right, honey," she said. "I know you will."

***

One day at the eye doctor's she had the assistant in stitches. First, her feet didn't touch the footrest and she was hamming it up, swinging them front to back. The woman finally had to clamp both hands over her mouth so the doctor wouldn't hear her giggling. "I'm not being very professional," she said.

When the doctor came in, we all looked at him soberly. "What's new?" he asked. "Not much," Mom said. "We're quiet people."

He laughed. "You sound like Louisa May Alcott," he said.

She loved to make people laugh, to leave places a little happier than she found them.

***

My boss' father died suddenly of a heart attack one day in October. My boss was shaken, of course, and rushed home to comfort his mother. Four days later, following the funeral for his father, his mother collapsed and died in his arms.

Too much to contemplate.

My boss saw the gift in the fact that his mother, suffering from diabetes, nearly blind, would not be alone. I told him I could almost see his father standing a few feet away, saying, "I waited so we could go together."

I wished for myself the same quick end when Lucy went. People told me that was wrong; that my life would not be over; that I would be 'free' to do whatever I wanted. Whatever could I want to do that would mean more to me than Lucy's smile?

***

Wordsworth spoke of "thoughts that lie too deep for tears." I had thoughts that lay too deep for words. I couldn't bring myself to express them; they were too painful.

She went through a phase in which she believed we had another house. Then one Sunday, she awoke from a nap and asked, "Where's Pam?" From that day on, she remained convinced that there was another Pam – "the other one," or "my Pam."

Sometimes they blamed her confusion on her retention of carbon dioxide; sometimes on the syndrome called "sun-downing." I wondered if it was the result of her head injury and maybe a little fluid on the brain. Whatever the cause or definition, the cruel reality of dementia had come to call.

For a time, the confusion would pass and she would be fine for a little while. "In a few minutes, she'll be back to herself and we'll laugh about this," I told myself. It was true—until it wasn't.

***

At about 8:30 a.m. one day she called me at work. She felt weak and very tired, she said. "I miss you so much." I was afraid to ask who she thought I was. It was enough that she missed me.

"Will you dress me up?" she asked. She had a doctor's appointment but was too weak to get ready. "Yes, my dear mother," I wanted to say. "I will wash you and clean your teeth and comb your hair and dress you up. I will learn to do what needs to be done and ease whatever hurts I can. I will do it to keep you with me, no matter how hard, how ugly, how exhausting it gets. But if your mind slips away, and with it the memory of us together, what is the point? Give me a reason to do it, Mom. Give me a reason to go on."

"Of course," I said.

***

Early one morning, she woke me by talking to herself; wishing aloud that she was in her own house. She was.

"Do we have a husband?" she asked. "Do we have any guy? No? Just the two of us?" She was disappointed but resigned.

Then, looking at me with her bright eyes: "What are you going to do with the kitty, Mommy?" My insides tightened. I tried to convince her that *I* was *her* daughter. She accused me of playing a game. "I don't know who you really are, but you sure in hell aren't my daughter."

I cried all night, not knowing if this cloud on her mind and memory would ever lift again. I couldn't bear the pain of watching her disintegrate mentally as well as physically. Earlier that day, before she got so muddled, she had said, "I tried so hard to get better, but I'm not going to get better."

That night for the first time, I prayed that she would die. I was ready to lose her rather than have her this way. The strongest person I ever knew was forced to cling to a bar while I washed her weary body. The brightest, funniest, most charming person I ever knew was convinced she was living in someone else's house with someone else's daughter.

***

In 1998, she was in Baystate for nine or 10 days in April and for another several days in May. Then, pressed by her doctor and my friends, I admitted her to a nursing home in Northampton. I reasoned that I would be able to visit her after work every day.

It was an absurd choice. We were 20 miles apart. Moreover, the care was terrible. There was not enough staff. I would find her trying to walk the halls while tethered to an oxygen tank. The doctor in charge was overbearing, wore a gold chain, and ignored my input.

It was supposed to be a permanent placement but she was so unhappy—we were so unhappy—that I brought her home. The day I went to pick her up, they gave me some nonsense. The doctor was reluctant to sign her out because she had a slight respiratory infection. I pitched a fit and a short time later, we were on our way.

Belted into the car, slumped slightly to the side, she looked unspeakably fragile. I asked her how she felt. She answered with one word. "Elated."

***

I hired a home health aide for 35 hours a week. We settled into the new routine—with a stranger in our home for several hours each day.

It was surreal. There was a DNR order taped to the refrigerator. I left detailed instructions; about Depends and wipes, about sponge baths and Brita pitchers. *Lucy will go from the chair to the bed and back about 100 times a day. She keeps her shoes on even when she lies down. She feels less afraid that way. She watches television all day. The soap operas help her to measure time. She knows I come home during* General Hospital. *She may pick up the phone and start pushing buttons at random. You can try to distract her or offer to help her make the call. The list of memory buttons is on the phone. She mostly will want to talk to me or to Ruth, our friend, who loves Lucy.*

And so it went.

***

In May 1999, she weighed about 117; her flesh, like her clothes, hung off her bones. She was still cute, still endearing most of the time. Other times she was combative and frightening to me because she was not my Lucy.

I missed my mother. I missed her companionship and her humor and her insights. I missed being able to jump into the car with her and take off for the day. I was tired of the oxygen tanks, the latex gloves, the cream for her sores; the eye drops. I was so sick of both the sameness and the fear of what tomorrow would bring.

***

In September 1999, she said, tears in her eyes, her fists clenched, "I want to be all strong." One night when she soiled herself, she cried. I had no words to comfort her.

***

The morning of Dec. 13, 1999, at 4:30, she sat with her chin resting on her chest and her eyes closed, and said softly, "I wish you could take me in your arms and fly me to heaven."

I wished that, too. But when she went to heaven, on Nov. 23, 2000, she went alone.

The obituary in the Gazette began:

Lucia (DeFlorio) Robbins Cummings, 84, of Springfield, mother of former Gazette staffer Pam Robbins, died Nov. 23 in ... Chicopee.

Born May 11, 1916, in Springfield, she was the daughter of the late Michael and Josephine (Desimone) DeFlorio.

She attended Springfield schools, graduating from the High School of Commerce, and later attended Springfield Technical Community College.

She had worked for the 3M Corp. in Springfield before retiring. She previously had worked for Technicolor, Standard Photo Service, the A&P, and Shea's Cleaners, all in Springfield.

She was a communicant of St. Mary's Church in East Springfield. She enjoyed tole painting and gardening and had been an avid reader....

It did not say that she was my heart.

***

Chapter Six: Her Own Words

After she was gone, I began the agonizing task of going through her drawers and closet. I found two things that made me weep. One was an envelope containing a smaller envelope, and inside that, a sheet of yellow legal paper. She had handwritten a poem that began: "When I am gone, do not grieve for me … ." She left it to comfort me. I imagine her at our dining-room table, carefully copying it from whatever source.

The second thing—her second gift—was a letter, 30-plus pages, a kind of autobiography, also handwritten, this time in pencil on the back of U.S. Census forms. We had both worked for the 1980 Census.

With minor editing, this is some of what she wrote to me.

Even now, after so many years I can see my mother's kitchen. It looked like a box—the kind you drew in kindergarten with two windows and three doors, the old water tank heater in the corner of the kitchen, the long shelf over the sink—the exposed sink with pipes showing and the inevitable set tub beside it. Its only claim to beauty was the oilcloth on the kitchen shelf over the sink that my father used to buy in the 5 &10 store. No matter that it matched nothing, any color served. But it was brand-new every year or so.

I can still see my father with his hammer and nails tacking it in place and then the placing back of the ornaments, ... the three jelly glasses, the Dutch cleanser, the bills, the medicine, the old bureau mirror streaked with water spots, and the comb.

The reason I have to describe the kitchen was because this was the room used more than any other room in the house. With one bathroom and 12 people this is where we washed up, combed and washed our hair. It was an ugly kitchen!

Now to tell you about the family that lived there.

There was Mama. Mama was a very big woman—about 5 ft. 2 and about 260 lbs. ... (She was) heavily lined and yet you could see the tracks of the beauty she must have had at one time. It's only now I can see she had beautiful features—straight nose and beautiful structured bones in her face, high cheekbones and beautiful brown-black hair, very little gray. It was the one thing she was vain about. She washed it every week and when she couldn't, due to health, used to beg whomever to do it for her.

Life treated her very shabbily, indeed. She never had a woman's world—the dreams she had were stepped on and crushed years before.

...

I will have to now give you a picture of my father. My father was a fat short man in his younger years—very good-looking with black hair and blue-gray eyes and very fair skin. ... There was more money on my father's side. He had to leave Italy because he got one of my grandmother's servants pregnant. It was not planned that he remain here but he did.

My mother came here around age 15 and moved in with an aunt. ... My mother worked hard to bring her three sisters Ida, Antoinette and Virginia, here and her two brothers, Jim and Frank.

I did not know any of the aunts on my father's side; he was the only son; I think he had two sisters. I was named after one of them. I know very little about my father's parents. They were better off than my mother's. My grandmother was a midwife and very smart and she had cancer of the breast. My grandfather was a shoemaker.

On my mother's side my grandfather was a musician and died at 36 and left six children. My grandmother died I guess in her 60s (pneumonia). ... I don't remember her hugging or ever kissing me.

As a child I felt close to my Uncle Frank. My Uncle Jim on the other hand I didn't like. He looked and was very much like my brother Joseph. They (Jim and Frank) were both barbers at first; they were in business together and then they split up. I didn't know too many of the details.

... Uncle Frank was very tall and had brown hair and big blue eyes, and a wonderful laugh. In his own way he tried to be good to me. After a fire at our house he came to school and took me home for the day. I remember his wife Maria putting me to bed in a high feather bed and I felt so great. It was so clean and fresh and I slept all day and then they fed me and he took me back to my home. Why he favored me I don't know, but I was happy and loved him when I was small.

In later years he had a nervous breakdown—not crazy or anything like that, just could barely cope with life, timid and withdrawn. ...

*My Uncle Jim ... died at the city hospital after a long illness. What (from) I don't know. I never went to see him—not from dislike. I was in prison myself (*a reference to her abusive second husband*) and only had a work pass, didn't have a go-visit-the-sick pass. ....*

My mother had 12 children, four died—her first two sons as infants and a daughter, Millie, at 13, and Harold. He fell from the second-floor porch on Marble Street after he had just come home from the hospital because he had his tiny arm mangled in a washing machine roller. He was just beautiful. He's the one I wrote the poem about.

"Eyes of blue, forget-me-nots.

Hair of golden grown

Lips that wore a sweet gay smile

Full of life was Harold!

Etc."

He was 2 or 2_, I believe. I was about 11. I was heart broken because I loved him. He would have been the baby of the family.

About my sister Millie who died at 13 from a cyst on her spine—I just remember dimly. I was a baby at the time. But I do remember the coffin in the living room—it was gray, and the cat that perched underneath and wouldn't leave until they took her out and that's all I can tell you.

Our living-room was quite nice. We had a piano, which in those days was no mean feat; mahogany set with green plush cushions; bamboo rack, four shelves and some very nice vases and mirrors and bric-a-brac. I believe my father more so than my mother loved beauty. He was more of a dandy. He used to dress to go to the club like some men dress for business ....

Something he said to me before he died was he would have liked to stay home ... and run the house. He found it difficult to cope with the working world. He was timid and gentle. I know I took after him but I had to cope, which quality I inherited from my mother. It was hard and I hated it.

From what I heard I was a beautiful child. I was very fair with brown curly hair. I know when I was probably 5 or 6, this prostitute, who at that time was my godfather's mistress, loved me and was very good to me. Took me places and loved to show me off. I loved my godfather very much and he, me. I guess he was in the Mafia because he showered me with expensive gifts. He was very handsome as only an Italian can be—tall, broad shoulders, curly hair and blue eyes and very macho. As I remember I only knew him as a child, then I didn't know what happened to him or his mistress. Funny I never forgot him—I guess because he returned my love.

...

At a very young age I discovered books and this set a pattern for the rest of my life. I loved that world because it was so much kinder and nicer than the one I was actually living in. ... Basically I never received the love I gave my family. Sometimes I wondered if I belonged. I don't know what the problem was.

I excelled at sports when I was a kid and loved camp life and still love the outdoors. As a kid I got along very well with people even though I preferred a book. My appearance hurt me in high school. We were damn poor. My clothing must have been absurd—the same skirt and Dan's sweater. He was a Springfield College student working at camp during the summers I went. He gave me his college sweater with the stripe on the sleeve. I wore it for years. ... He was my friend. He used to write articles for the paper on doings at the camp. I always got three-quarters of the articles written about me.

I loved camp and it was the only happy time of my childhood. I ate three good meals a day and I was respected and loved, and in charge. I know now that given a different set of circumstances I would have been somebody.

I was graduated from high school at a young age because I skipped a whole grade. Looking back I wish they hadn't done this because I missed a lot of basics. At Howard Street School in the sixth grade I had the highest IQ of anyone. Teachers made a big to-do about it and the kids looked and regarded me with awe.

Then when I went to State Street Junior High I started to go downhill. Things started to close in on me—the terribly unhappy home life, the poverty, lack of good food, and those awful clothes. Kids used to make fun of my lunches so I wouldn't eat lunch any more. I used to sit in my homeroom. My grades started to go down and nobody cared.

It wasn't until my second year of high school that they realized I couldn't see the board or read a lot of stuff. I used to bring the notices home from school that my eyesight was bad. No one cared. Finally the school nurse took me to Dr. Donovan and chipped in and bought me my first pair of glasses and they also sent a food basket. I was so shamed I didn't want to go back to school. ... When I got my glasses I acted like Johnny Belinda. I could see! The whole world looked so different. I needed glasses since third grade. I missed a lot by not having them.

... I don't know who my drummer was but he gave me a rough time. I can't really describe myself. Good worker, loyal, loads of compassion and very innocent. When I felt loved or secure I could excel. If not, I would put my four sides around me and act like a lump.

After graduation, 1934, there were no jobs. The family was on welfare at the time. My older brother got tired of working at the city yard so he ran away and left us. At that that time you had to work out your aid so my brother Larry went to CC camps and I went ironing at the City Home. Great for a 17-year-old kid—plus the insults from the welfare social worker at that time, who wouldn't give me carfare ... because she told me I was fat and the walk would do me good. She made this remark in front of a whole roomful of people. There is honor among the poor; no one laughed except the bitch. Even now I feel the hurt and rage.

... It was an unhappy period, my so-called youth. All those lousy jobs—cannery for WPA where you stuffed food in cans, NYA where I worked in the schools taking care of pre-kindergarten children. ... I used to bring home leftover food from the nursery and school in these big tin containers. It made my mother happy.

I always had too many responsibilities. I was nervous and felt I deserved none of the good things of life. ... I would have loved a little room like yours. To be able to close a door, what heaven that would have been. ... .

As a kid I adored my family but they used me in every shabby way they could. ..

... Given a decent job, a little love and kindness then things would have fallen into place. I treat my cat and dog better than I was treated by my family I was my own worst enemy. Because I had a good heart. ...

... I'll never forget ... I had taken the bus downtown to visit M. .... My mother called and M. told her I was there. She, my mother, said, "Throw her out – (she's) Miss Poison." ... I left and cried all the way home on the bus. They had finally broken me. Then my mother would tell other members of the family not to have me because I ate too much. ... She did an awful job on me... ... It wasn't until her 60s she took the big turnabout; all of a sudden I became top man. She found out what frauds they all were. By then I was in my late 30s and it was too late. ... The hurts were too deep.

I know this is confusing to you because I never told you how I really felt. At least you were loved all your life. I don't really think I want to see them on the other side. I was a victim because I allowed myself to be—because I loved and believed and people took advantage of me. So now I can't feel compassion for them. Years ago I learned to live alone and how to handle it. They can't cope with it now and frankly I don't give a damn. I will send their stupid cards but they won't ever get a part of me again. What helped were books. Saved my sanity. ...

My marriage to your father I won't go into too much because you know most of this. He was rotten. It was 12 years of hell. Bob (her second husband) *...forget it. Hell! Hell! Hell!*

You were the only person I had left to love. I know I spoiled you and gave in to your whims but you were a good girl and a good daughter.

She signed it, and dated it, Jan. 1, 1982.

Chapter Seven: The Background

Though she tried to hide it, I felt the undercurrent of my mother's pain all my life. My father, whom she loved deeply, left us when I was about 5. I have a memory of him lifting me up and my face brushing the string that hung from the overhead light in the kitchen. I think that happened the day he left, but I may have created that notion later.

I do remember sitting on the porch steps, looking down the street; I thought he had gone to the store. At some point, I must have realized he was not coming home, and so I clung to my mother.

I have, I think, two or three greeting cards and a cheap gold-plated bracelet by which to remember him—those things and a lifetime of feeling not good enough.

Because my father never paid his child support, and left my mother in debt, she was forced to take in boarders for a while. Too proud to go on welfare, she went to work. Gradually, she dragged us to higher financial ground. She began improving the house—a new sink, a chain-link fence. Things were fine until she was introduced to the antichrist who, some seven years later, would become her second husband.

What she did not know was that for several of those years—from the time I was 5 or 6, until I was about 10, that man molested me on a regular basis. This is such an old and tired story now that it hardly bears repeating—except that it damaged my personality and destroyed my potential. His negotiating tool to ensure my secrecy? "If your mother finds out, she will hate you."

The abuse stopped when I was old enough and strong enough to stop it. But I did not tell. Then, when I was nearly 13, my mother lost her job and in the face of that challenge, she agreed to marry him. I begged her not to, but she thought it was a case of my having had all her attention for so long, being reluctant to share her. She was sure it would all work itself out.

They wed on my 13th birthday. I did not attend. He wanted to adopt me—insane as he was—but I balked enough that he settled for guardianship. What followed were eight years of torture as victims of his control, his verbal, emotional onslaughts and his violent outbursts. He played us against each other: If I stood up to him, he went after her and vice versa.

So we lived a cowed existence as he systematically broke down our egos and our confidence. I remember kneeling on the kitchen floor, stacking his beer bottles in the refrigerator just the way he liked them. I remember a girl from high school stopping by one Christmas, wondering why I was acting so odd because she did not know that he was hiding in the cellar, monitoring our conversation. I remember that when he went up to bed, my mother and I pantomimed or wrote notes to each other, lest he grow angry that we were enjoying each other's company.

Of course, my mother regretted her decision to marry him. She begged him to leave. He would not. How could we force him? The one battle she fought and won was her refusal to put his name on her house. That act of defiance saved us later.

In 1965, before my senior year of college, I went away for several weeks of officer candidate training, preparing to be commissioned a Marine Corps second-lieutenant at graduation. A recruiter had come to my college and offered me a summer away, and the promise of a career as a part of something meaningful. I had tried to enter religious life earlier and had been turned down. So this was a dream come true.

The candidate course restored some of my sense of self-worth and when I came home to finish school, I was deeply conflicted. On one hand, the U.S. Marine Corps said I was fit to be an officer. On the other, my stepfather said I was an imbecile and a loser, and did not hesitate to remind me of that. Dissonant messages in spades.

A couple of weeks before graduation, he and I got into an argument, in the course of which I approached hysteria and blurted out what he had done to me when I was a child. My mother collapsed into a chair as the blood drained from her face. She was stunned. "You can't stay," she said to him. He refused to go and I unleashed a stream of obscenities and threats. We called the police but he took them aside and they exchanged the Knights of Columbus handshake, or something, and the next thing I knew, they were glaring at me and climbing into their cruiser. God knows what he told them.

Simply put, he did not go gracefully. But he went, and she filed for divorce. When the time came to serve him with the papers, we could not find anyone with the courage to accompany the sheriff as required. I went. I also flew home from active duty to testify at the divorce hearing. "Congratulations," the judge said, sarcastically. "You helped your mother get divorced. You should be very proud."

(Years later, my stepfather would follow us around in his car, darting around corners to frighten us. The police could do nothing: This was long before anti-stalking laws. So I called a lawyer and asked for his help. Because I was 20-something and ridiculously naïve, I told him I thought he could do something because he was reputed to have Mafia ties. He laughed. "That's just a rumor," he said.

My stepfather's harassment stopped. I called to thank the lawyer. I could tell he was smiling when he said, "All I did was write him a letter. He must have heard the same rumors you did.")

For my mother, two marriages, one worse than the other, were piled upon the memories of a childhood in which she had felt loved and valued too little.

Small wonder that my heart ached for her; that I longed to make things right for her. Not surprising that when she died, I felt I had lost not only my mother, my friend and my companion, but also my fellow survivor.

Chapter Eight: The Passing

Less than two months after Lucy's death, I began making daily recordings that later were transcribed and edited. What follows are excerpts of those recordings, which sketch the story of my first year of grieving. They are written as they were spoken to her—in present tense.

Hi, Mom. Today is January 12, 2001. It's a Friday. It's five days before my 56th birthday, and I'm standing at your grave, and wishing that we were together. It's inconceivable to me that you've been dead seven weeks and one day. No one will ever know how lost I am without you.

I'm speaking into a little recording device that I bought. I know that nobody really wants to hear me talk about you morning, noon, and night. And I need to, because it's as if part of me has been amputated.

I'd like to write something about you someday, about losing you. Maybe it would help someone else who loves someone so much that they can't imagine living without them.

***

It's Saturday, January 13, about 2 o'clock in the afternoon. In a little while I'll go up to Northampton to have dinner with Annie. I wish that I could go home and find you there, happy to see me, and then we would have the evening together. I miss you young, when you came down the street carrying the groceries and I ran to meet you, and I miss you old, asleep in your chair, your hands clasped in your lap. You'd open your eyes, smile, "Hi, Honey."

A couple of weeks before you died, you put your hand on my face and, totally lucid, you said, "Oh, my dear girl, there was so much I wanted to give you." The truth is that you gave me more than any mother ever gave a daughter. I wouldn't have made it without you. I wouldn't make it now without you. I only hope I get to see you again.

I long to cry but some days I'm too numb to cry.

It seems like yesterday that I left a client's office and called the nursing home, thinking they were going to say you were fine. I was going to say, "Well, tell her I'll see her in a little while." Instead Jan, the unit manager, said, "Yeah, she's not doing well," and I said, "I'm on my way."

"Drive carefully," she said, and all the way over I knew that this was it.

When I got there, you were in bed, and everyone looked very sad. They told me that a student from an LPN program had gone in to get you up, about 8 or 8:30, and you were unresponsive. The doctor later said that you had stroked, which is what I had suspected.

The last time I heard you speak was when two aides went in to clean you up. As they were turning you, you seemed so flaccid, so changed, that I just couldn't believe it. Then you said, "Ow!" and someone said, "We're sorry, Lucy," and you said, "OK." That was the last word I ever heard you say. "OK."

I peeked through the corner of the curtain and saw one aide, Audrey, bend down and kiss your forehead.

Later, your roommate told me that she could swear she had heard you call my name the night you stroked. That's one of the things that haunts me—that you called my name and I wasn't there. I wonder if you became afraid; if you felt yourself drifting and called for me, because I had been your anchor, as you had been mine. I'm sorry I wasn't there.

***

It's still Saturday, and it's 4 o'clock, and I'm sitting outside Annie's apartment. I'm early and I'm thinking that I'm sorry I wasn't more patient with you. I'm sorry that I got upset and angry, and mean and mean-spirited. You deserved none of that. I wish I could go back and do it again. I wish I could do it knowing how little time there was left to do it.

It's about 9:30 now, and I can't stop thinking about you. I was remembering some of the things we said those last couple of weeks in the nursing home. Once you looked at me with your sad, sick eyes, and said, "I don't know how much more of this I can stand." I said, "Well, I just want you to be happy and at peace, Mom. You do what you need to do."

You searched my face. "Yeah?" Then you nodded. "OK."

Another time I said, "I'll always love you," and you replied, "I'll always love *you*." I said, "I was only happy when I was with you, Mommy." You said, "Me, too." Then I said, "But one of us is going to have to leave the other soon," and you replied, "I know that." Then we sat quietly for a long time, holding hands, knowing.

I don't know why I couldn't have died the same day you did. It would have been a blessing for me. But I'm here, and I'm going to try to do what you'd want me to do: get the house in order, sell the things that don't matter, keep the things that do. I don't know where I'll end up, but this house is not a home any more. It's just a building without you.

You wanted to go home—you told me a hundred times. I think you meant a time, not a place. I'm sitting in our house, looking at your empty chair, and all of the life and light has gone out of this room. As much as you wanted to go home, I want to go home, and I have as little chance. The only way I'll go is when I leave this earth. I hope I'll find you, because home is where you are.

I burn a candle in front of your picture every night that I can, a way of letting you know that I'm thinking of you, a way of showing you honor and respect. I'm comforted by the fact that Jesus said to the good thief, "Today you will be with me in paradise." So there must be a paradise, and if there is, then I know you're there.

***

Today is Sunday. It's January 14, three days before my birthday. I want to tell you about the day that you died.

It was Thanksgiving Day, as you well know. I got to the nursing home about 7:30, and went into the shower room where you were resting. People think it strange that you died in a shower room, but Jan had you moved there the previous night because the lady in the next bed had a lot of company and we wanted it to be quiet for you. There was an open area and some shower stalls. Your bed was in the open area; no one took showers for the time you were there.

It was very peaceful there, right next to the nurses station, and I hope you could hear the phones, and the murmur of voices and footsteps. Those sounds were familiar to you because you used to sit right there. The visitors would walk by and most would wave to you and say, "Hi, Lucy," and "'Bye, Lucy."

So there you were in the shower room, resting quietly. I kept waiting for you to begin gasping and thrashing and all of the things I had been warned about, but that never happened.

Annie joined me, and we took up our vigil. You got more and more quiet, and your respirations became slower. About 4 or 5 o'clock, Gloria and Evie came and sat for a little while, and sometime between 4 and 6—I'm not quite sure of the times or the intervals—you laughed, three times. We were stunned the first time, thrilled the second and third, wondering what you were seeing. Were there people you loved there? Were they joking with you? What was happening that so delighted you? All of us laughed with you.

All day, I kept telling you it would be OK, that you would be welcomed when you went, that it would be wonderful. I hope I was telling the truth.

About 7 or 8 o'clock, I went out and got the pulse oxymeter and put it on your finger to measure your oxygen saturation. I had been seeing 80s and 70s and I thought, oh now it'll show a 50, and there'll be this kind of gradual drop. But, in fact, I could not even get a reading, and I knew that we were down to the wire. Your feet began to get very cold, and I knew you were dying.

During that day, some of the other patients' family members came in. One old man named Harry, who used to tease you, made his way on a walker. He stood at the door and said, "I feel bad. She was a lot of fun." I guess that's pretty much how I'd sum it up, too.

Finally, Roz, the aide you liked so much, showed up. She came in although it was her day off. It was 8 o'clock in the evening, and she had to get a ride, because someone had her car. She brought her son, who sat in the TV room, and she came to sit with us.

Suddenly some dark fluid came out of your mouth and nose. It was as if you had taken charcoal and then spit up. You didn't react to it very much. Roz jumped up with a towel and told me to get a nurse.

I ran out and called Eileen, who was doing her med pass. Brian, the handsome young aide and nursing student, was standing at the foot of the bed, and I remember he didn't quite meet my eyes until he had gathered himself a bit, and then he looked at me, and I said, "Is she gone?" and he said, "Yeah."

Eileen put her stethoscope on your chest, and confirmed it: "She's gone." I said, "Can we take off the oxygen?" and she said yes. You were on five liters at that point, so it was noisy and it was nice to have it turned off. I asked that they call three people: the director of nursing, a minister I knew, and Jan. I went downstairs and called Gloria from the payphone. She asked if I wanted her to come. I said no, that I'd need her over the next few days, but not now.

Then I went back upstairs and sat in the room, and Annie and I cried. We continued singing and reading to you, and telling you goodbye, because some traditions teach that the soul remains for a while. Brian said, "I'd like to be the one to get her ready, if that's OK." He and a young woman bathed you very gently and she said, "We're going to make you smell as fresh and clean as a baby, Lucy," and kissed you.

By the time they were through, you looked peaceful, regal, and so frail—a little woman who had fought so hard to stay with her daughter.

The minister said a prayer and Annie and I and several staff joined hands. Then I said the funeral home could come for you.

And so you were gone.

I was with you that day from 7:30 in the morning, until you died, and for an hour beyond that. I told you everything I thought you should know. I said goodbye a hundred times. I said I was sorry a hundred times. I hope you heard me.

For the record, you died November 23 in the year 2000, at 8:55 p.m. Your death was as peaceful as I could have wished for you. I only wish we could have spoken one or two more words to each other.

The funeral was unremarkable. The priest you liked celebrated the Mass and gave a nice sermon. He told me to call if I needed him.

***

I never thought that someone could be so empty and go on living.

Chapter Nine: Regrets

Today is Tuesday, January 16, 2001. There are so many things that I regret every day, and that I weep over every night.

I regret that I didn't quit my job sooner and stay home with you. I regret that when you were in the hospital that October, and I decided to bring you home, I had the home health aide come back. That was a big mistake. That was my opportunity to take six months off and spend them with you. I think you would have been more content then, and I would be more at peace now.

I regret that you could not die at home, although I don't regret choosing the nursing home I chose. It was not prepossessing at all, but Jan was there. You loved her and she seemed to care for you. I saw the kindness in her eyes the night she kneeled by your chair in the hall and held your hand while you dozed.

So I regret that I didn't stay home. I didn't know what to do. I didn't want to run out of money. I remembered how hard you fought not to go on welfare when Daddy left. You scrimped and did without, so that I could have a little nest egg, and I didn't want to squander it. So I felt I had to keep working.

The only person who could ever help me make a decision was you, and you were no longer able to help. I was so tired, so overwhelmed, and so terrified that I didn't know what to do.

I regret that I yelled at you so much; that I was so angry, so unkind. But that didn't happen in the course of a normal day. It happened at 10 at night or 2 in the morning when you were trying to go out the back door with your walker and your oxygen cord, or you were hysterical because you could not find Pam and I was begging you to understand that I was Pam. I was running around showing you pictures of us together, pointing to my face. "I know," you kept saying, "but I want the other Pam. PAM, PAM," you would yell up the stairs.

It happened when you would wake me every two hours, every hour, every half-hour, and I was so desperate and so tired and I just wanted you to lie down or sit down for an hour.

So if I was impatient or ill-tempered, or I disappointed or frightened you ever, it wasn't willful. Still, I will bear the pain of having done it for the rest of my life.

I hope that you remember the loving moments, too; when I would give you a shower and wash your hair and put you in clean clothes. I'd walk you to the chair and cover you with an afghan and comb your beautiful white hair, and say, "There. You smell like a flower and you look so pretty." And you'd smile. I'd make your seafood-salad sandwich and give you a glass of cranberry juice with lots of ice, or a cup of tea. Maybe you'd have an apple square or ice-cream that I had brought home earlier. I never went anywhere or did anything that I didn't think of you and what I could do to make you happy.

It's 9:30 p.m. I was just looking at the cards that I got for my birthday. The card I used to take most for granted was yours; now that's the card I would most like to see.

I talked to Christie from the nursing home, today. She mentioned that she has been battling cancer for three years. If I had known, I would have told you and, as long as you could have held the thought in your head, you would have felt bad for her.

I found some letters that you wrote me when I was in the Marine Corps. In one, you told me I'd never have anything to reproach myself for. But you wrote that when I was 20 or 21. A lot happened between then and the day you died, and I wonder if you still could have said that. I hope so, but I wonder.

I threw away a lot of your old checks, your old statements. I went to the bank and closed our joint savings account. It was mostly your money—money that you saved painstakingly for me.

I see my main work now as getting ready to die: to get things in order for when I move on. I hope we're reunited then. That's all I'm clinging to.

Today marked the 50th day that I've gone to the cemetery. I pledged to go for 49 days because I once read that Buddhists believe the soul stays with the body for 49 days, and I didn't want you to be lonely. Tomorrow I plan to start going five days a week instead of seven. I don't know if I can stop. In many ways it's been the glue that's held me together. I miss you so much.

In your letters, you mentioned missing me more than you ever thought you would. Only I knew how much you needed me. I still need you. I weep at night because I think if you could help me, you would. For some reason you can't. That breaks my heart because I don't want you to be frustrated or sad in heaven. I say that, and people think I'm crazy. Maybe I am. But it's the way I feel.

***

It's January 17 at about 7 in the morning, It's my 56th birthday; the first I've had to spend without my mother. Even when I was in the Marine Corps, I tried to be home for my birthday. I just lighted a candle in front of your picture, to honor you for all that you did for me—all the happy birthdays that you gave me, all the support and love.

I was remembering that time I was working as a freelancer, I believe it was back in the '70s, and I used to have panic attacks. I'd be out in the middle of the night tromping around in the snow in the backyard trying to work off the adrenaline rush. You'd put on your old green jacket, put your hands in your pockets and walk with me.

I can remember when I'd lie on my bed and shake from pure anxiety, and you would sit on the edge of the bed and wrap your strong arms around my legs and hold them. "There, honey, it's OK. Mommy's here."

I'm sorry you're not with me today. I hope you're having a happy day.

***

Hey, Mom, it's January 18 at 10:34 p.m. Gloria spent the day with me today and we looked at markers for your grave. I found one—beautiful and simple just like you. I'm going to order it. I think I may order mine at the same time, so we will have matching stones.

I had a pretty nice birthday this year, all things considered. My friends were very nice to me. But to come home at the end of it and not have you to tell it all to makes everything seem hollow. Without you my world is a little dark and bleak all the time.

You were the best friend I'll ever have. You were my companion, my comforter, my advocate, my defender. You were everything to me. The director of nursing at the home said that in her years of experience, she's never seen a staff behave so tenderly at a death. To me, it says something about how wonderful you were.

I sure could use a message from you, Lucy. I need something to tell me that you're OK and that you still love me and that we'll meet again.

***

Good morning, Mom. It's January 19 at about 6:45 or 7 o'clock. I go to bed sad, and I wake up sad. I wish I could sleep for 20 hours a day, because it's only when I'm sleeping that I don't miss you. No matter what I'm doing, there's a big hole in my heart.

I was hoping that as soon as you were safely home, I would go. I had a vision of myself running through the tunnel they talk about and yelling, "Mommy, wait for me, I'm coming too." It was a happy picture. The thing is that the longer I'm alive, the more frightened I become of dying. Yet, given a choice between going on like this for 20 or 30 years, and being with you today, I'd rather be with you.

We have some freezing rain, which means not only that I will not get to the cemetery, but also that Annie will be driving on icy roads, which worries me terribly. She's such a sad girl sometimes. But maybe there are better things coming for her; I hope so. I hope she gets the brass ring. Some of us just don't ever seem to get what we hope for or expect or deserve. You were certainly the prime example of that.

I wanted you to know that Joe T's wife called last night. He died four years ago. I guess I didn't know that, or if I did, I had forgotten. She saw your obit and called to tell me that whenever she has company she thinks of you because she uses the sugar bowl and creamer that you gave her. She said that every time they used to drive by our house they wondered how you were. That was nice to know.

I don't think I told you that I ran into one of my cousins the other day as I was leaving Baystate and she said that your older brother is in intensive care. He's 86 and very sick so I don't know if he's going to be joining you soon or what.

What a sad thing for you to have had seven siblings and so little contact and so little comfort. One of them never even sent me a Mass card or sympathy card. I can't believe how cold that was. I can't believe they didn't see what a treasure you were.

I miss you. It was eight weeks yesterday to the day. I hope God lets us be together. I hope that's what heaven is.

It's 2:30, and the guy from the gas company is supposed to come and do a final read on the meter and then they will change the account to my name. It's very hard for me to take these steps, Lucy.

I got a card today via Ruth from her pen-pal who lives in Connecticut. It talks about the spirits and what they do when people die. It says that they whisper, "Don't miss me too much; the view is nice and I'm doing just fine." I wonder if this was a message from you. I can hear you saying it.

I am missing you so much. It's a visceral, relentless pain. I look at your pictures and I want to run screaming down the street. I go through drawers and boxes of your papers praying I'll find something that will give me some peace. I wish we could have had some closure. I wish we could have had a moment—clear and unequivocal; that you could have looked into my eyes and said, "Goodbye, Pam. I love you."

But I'm not complaining, because at least your death was quiet and peaceful and maybe if you'd been conscious you would have struggled more to stay. You would have seen my need for you and tried to meet it. That's what you always did.

You were the bravest, truest and most decent person I ever knew. Anything I've ever done right I did because of you, because of your example and your strength. I don't know what's going to become of me, Lucy. I don't know if I can make a life.

You were such a paradox, so edgy and funny and yet so vulnerable. "Let's all sing like the birdies sing," you said one night at the nursing home. I said, "Mommy, I don't know what you're talking about." I didn't understand, and you kept saying it with such intensity and frustration, "Let's all sing like the birdies sing!" It turned out to be a song and I found out later that Annie knew it and could have sung it to you.

I think that was only two or three days before you died. When you were dying we sang 'The Teddy Bear Song"; "My Buddy"; "Sleep My Child." I sang "Scarlet Ribbons"; said the "Our Father." We read the 23rd Psalm. We did everything we knew to do to make it better, easier for you.

I always hope that I'll dream about you. But I never do.

***

It's January 20, about 6 p.m. I did get to the cemetery today and I was happy about that, even though I couldn't stay too long. It was cold and lonely there.

The days go by so slowly and so sadly. I don't see much down the road for me, Mom. I'm lost. And I'm so alone.

I watched a lot of the President's inauguration today. I kept looking at your empty chair and thinking of how much fun we would have had watching it. You loved history and personalities and we would have had the best time. But it wasn't to be.

Oh, Lucy. I think of how brave you were all your life. How you just kept on going in the face of what seemed like insurmountable odds. You deserved so much more than you got. I wish I could have made your dreams come true.

I'm so sorry that I never, in those last 13 years, got you out of Springfield. You'd say, "*I'd* like to take a vacation." And I'd say, "Oh we will," but we never did. One time when I was reminding you of our trips to see the ocean, you said, "Make it happen again, honey." But I couldn't. I asked Jan when you were in the nursing home. She was firm: You wouldn't be able to handle the trip. Another regret: I waited too long.

I'm sorry I didn't ask more questions and listen harder to the answers. I'm sorry I didn't spend more time talking to you. I'm sorry that I didn't get rid of the aide five minutes after I saw that you disliked her. I'm sorry I kept working at a job I hated instead of staying home and caring for you. I'm sorry I didn't move us out of this house into a place where I could have taken care of you more easily and you wouldn't have been so frightened. Everybody says I did so much. I didn't do as much as you would have done if the situation had been reversed.

My heart is empty and my soul is numb. I don't understand how God expects me to go on without you. I think sometimes He asks too much of us.

***

Hi, Mom. It's Monday, I think it's January 22. I went to your grave today. I got snow in my boots but I was happy to be able to visit you. I'm trying to go about five times a week now because I can't keep going every day forever. I wish we had talked more about these things. I wish I had asked you what would be enough.

I've burned your candle all day today. I took out the picture of you when you were younger, and that's the one I'm looking at now as I talk to you. I hope you are somewhere, not just dead in the ground. I hope that what faith teaches is true. It seems that everyone in my life believes it except me. I can't seem to get ahold of it with my heart and I so need to believe you're somewhere.

I'm supposed to have lunch with Christie on Thursday. She's a kind person.

Annie's going to Florida for a week, so I'll be lonely when she's gone. Evie's birthday is Saturday. I need to get her a card. Remember when she put the handles up for you—one in the bathroom and one coming up onto the porch, and then one coming into the house? Those handles were such a blessing for you.

I look at your chair. I can see you sitting there with your head turned to the right. I can see the bruises on your hand as it rests on the arm of the chair. I can see your sneakers with your laces always coming untied. The sneaks are in my car now. I put them right where they would be if you were riding with me. Nobody understands why this matters, or why I need to wear your sweater and touch the places on the banister where you rested your hand. But these things are all I have left.

For so many years people said to me, "You need to get a life." I want to say to them, "I had a life. Lucy was my life and now she's gone. And now I have to build a new life out of nothing but the ashes of what we had together."

You were the dearest person. I was working today and I could just hear you say, "How you doing, honey? Are you almost done?" What a good mother and what a dear friend.

I thank you for all the times you were on my side when no one else was, all the times you put up with me and humored me and tolerated my moods. I know I wasn't easy: so much baggage, so many wounds, so troubled about so many things. I wouldn't have made it without your love. You kept me going, soothed me, comforted me. You gave me a reason to come home, a reason to go on living. I don't know where I'll find the reason now, or the strength.

I try to remember if I did anything to bring you really great joy. I never married or had a child, and those were the two things you wanted most from me, or for me, or both. But you saw me graduate from college and saw me be commissioned a Marine Corps officer wearing dress whites. You saw me win a writing award and have it presented to me at the Harvard Club in Boston. You saw me get my master's degree—and you saw me publish a book and sign a hundred copies in one day. Everyone paused to shake your hand and told you I was special. And that made you feel special, too. So I tried.

"My heart is very broken" you told me. My heart is very broken too, Mom, and the only thing that will heal it is to have you take my hand and bring me home.

***

Hi, Mommy. It's Tuesday. I'm not sure if it's the 22nd. I'm a little mixed up on the dates. I always miss you a lot at night. It's the time we used to settle down and keep each other company. Sometimes I feel your energy in the room, as if you're still here.

You made me laugh so much, Mommy – even when you became confused. One night we were watching TV and you looked at me and said, "Well, we might as well go to bed. These people are never going to go home."

When you were younger and healthier, I'd be in bed and I'd hear you get up during the night. I'd think, "Oh she's up, she's moving, she's OK, she's still with me."

What a gift, all the years I had with you. How lucky I was. I remember that stupid doctor who told me in 1969 that you had three months to three years to live. I lived with that terror for such a long time. I should have sued his sorry ass for the emotional distress he caused me. You fooled them, Mommy. You were supposed to be dead in 1970 and you lived 30 more years.

Once, much later, when you left the hospital after a severe bout of pneumonia, another doctor said, "Your mother won't be the same as she was before, you know. She's going to be kind of an invalid and you're going to have to adjust." I think you got out of the hospital in February and by April you were sawing down six pine trees and raking the yard. You wore that old green jacket when you did it. I'll keep that jacket until the day I die.

I treasure so many things that were part of you. They hold so much of your energy and so many memories for me. When I put on a sweater that you wore, it's as though I can feel your warmth encompassing me.

You were such a loving mother. In my baby book you wrote that my eyes were 'like the flash of sunlight on a bluebird's wings." I wonder if that was original or if you just quoted it. I'll never know. I wish I had your stories and your poems. I wish your brother hadn't thrown them away. How could he do that?

I understand why you'd say I was the only one you had to love. You were the only one I really had to love, too. Now there's just me and my memory of you.

***

Hi, Mom. It's Wednesday. I guess it's the 23rd of January. I just came from seeing the minister. I was telling her how I feel you were cheated by life. I never saw anybody try so hard and do the right thing so consistently and be hammered so consistently in return.

It's hard for me to understand where God was in that. I'm terrified that when I die I'll go to hell and so we won't be together. In fact, not being together would be hell enough for me.

I guess I don't understand why I can't get a clear message from you. But maybe that will come someday when I need it more. I can only hope.

You were the best mother I could have had, the best friend I ever had. I sit here surrounded by pictures of you but you're not here.

I'll be glad when it's spring and I can visit your grave and not have to run off because my feet are freezing. I try to go three to five times a week now, Mom. I'm trying to cut back, to talk to you more here in our house, in this room that I shared with you for 55 years.

***

Good morning, Mom. Today is Thursday. I think the date is January 24. I was thinking how I could always say, "Oh I can't because I have to take care of my mother. I have to go home to my mother. I don't leave my mother alone at night. I can't go." Now I have to say I just don't want to.

I saw Christie today. She said you were a special person, that everybody who came in contact with you loved you. I think that was true. I hope it was.

***

It's Friday night, almost 11 o'clock. I've had kind of a bad day. I went to Stop & Shop and remembered the day that I brought you there and it was really hot and you had your oxygen tank. I said, "You wait here. I'm just going to run in and get a couple of things and I'll be right out."

I went to the deli and then, as I was racing through the store, I was paged. I hurried to the front and there was a man there. He said, "Your mother flagged me down and asked me to tell you to come out." (You said to him, "Do you know my daughter, Pam Robbins?") So I went out and you were trying to make your way to the store, carrying your oxygen tank. "Hi, honey," you said, with a big smile.

Now I go into that store and I see the seafood salad and the eclairs and cranberry juice. Oh, how I miss you. I have a hole in my heart and nothing will ever fill it.

If I get healthy, if I have fun, if I'm happy, is that like betraying you? You would say of course not. But I don't know.

***

Hi, Mom. It's Saturday morning and I guess it's January 27 and I woke up with some kind of an aura and then a headache with a visual disturbance and it scared the hell out me. I was wishing that you were here to tell me that I'd be OK. When I think of you these days I don't think of you when you were most compromised. I think of you when you were in your 70s and still on top of everything and still strong enough to make me feel safe.

So it was kind of a scary morning and now I'm sitting here with a killer headache, and not feeling too well. I'm very sad.

I worry that when they gave you your inhaler at the nursing home they didn't give it to you right because they used to rush you. I think of all these things I might have done to prolong your life another week, another month. Maybe you wouldn't have stroked if you'd been in better shape when you were younger—maybe, maybe, maybe. I guess this must be part of the grief.

I talked to a nurse educator who's paid by the funeral home chain to do grief work with people. Her husband died when she was 31, and her son died and he was only 21. So she knows a lot about grief. She said it affects every part of your mind and body, every part of your life. She asked how long it had been since you died. I said eight weeks and she said, "Oh, you're just starting." So I guess I have a long haul ahead of me.

She understood that it's hard for me to go to the grocery store. I can't go into the bakery and look at the apple squares. I've yet to make myself French toast. If you can't have things anymore it's hard for me to enjoy them. I don't know what I'm going to do.

You knew what it was to live alone. I was telling Gloria today how, when I was in the Marine Corps, you were trying to paint the garage and you fell off a ladder. You lay there until Connie happened to come by and find you. She took you to Mercy Hospital.

I think of the time you fell in the driveway and hurt your hand and the time you got locked outside one cold morning, and the neighbor came over and popped the lock on the storm door to let you in. There were so many things that you just dealt with all by yourself. I'm sorry that you had such a hard time.

I tried to be there, but I know my response to things was not always right. I think it's because I felt your pain and I was so helpless and I got so angry. I'm so sorry. I wish I could have done more for you. The only thing I ever wanted was to be a good daughter to you, to make your life a little better. I hope I did that.

***

Hi, Mommy, it's Sunday night about 8:30. The stupid Super Bowl is on. If you were here, I would probably have rented a movie. I went to see Gloria and Evie today and looked at the apartment again--the one they want me to rent. Every time I look at it, I'm stunned by how small it is.

It's cold in the house. The cat isn't anywhere near, so I don't know what she's doing. I've gone through photo albums all weekend trying to sort through pictures and I ended up with 11 photo albums. What the hell I'm going to do with them I have no idea.

God asks too much, expecting us to go on when the one person we love is gone.

***

Hi, Mom. It's Monday, January 29. It's about 5 p.m. I've had one of those days of paralysis. I went through some papers and threw away some cards sent to you. Found a couple from Gloria, one of them saying, "If you ever need me, you know how to get a hold of me." I guess that was during the time she and I weren't speaking. It meant a lot to me that she kept in touch with you during that time. I think it meant a lot to you.

Aside from that and, you know, just kind of shuffling some papers and moving them from one pile to another, I didn't really accomplish anything today.

***

It's January 29 at about 11 p.m. I had dinner with Charlie and Kelly and Annie and it was nice. It would have been nicer if you'd been there. I talk about you as much and as often as I can to try to keep you alive.

***

It's Wednesday, January 31. It's about quarter to ten at night. Went to see Gloria and Evie tonight for supper and then hurried home. I was actually glad you weren't in the car because you would have been scared on those winding roads.

What I'll miss most is turning onto our street and seeing our house and knowing that I'm almost home. I remember walking home with you from the bus stop and we would say, "We're almost there, we're almost there." When we got to the brick houses, it was just a stone's throw and then we would be inside our warm little house, the place where we were safe from the world.

I remember you used to walk up the path in front of me. Then, as you got older and sicker, you'd hold on to my arm, or I'd hold on to yours, and I'd help you up that big step. Before it was over I was practically dragging you up the steps. Evie put the handle next to the door for you and you'd wrap your sturdy little hand around it and pull. You had quite a grip right till the end. You never gave up. You kept fighting until there was no more fight left in you. I've never seen anybody with such courage and such determination.

I miss that. I miss your sense of humor, your patience, your willingness to reach out time and time again. You were a good woman, Mom. You weren't perfect, but you were a good woman.

When you were dying, I told you that when you got to Heaven, God was going to say, "Lucy, you did such a good job with the life I gave you." It's true. You paid your taxes and raked your yard and drove the speed limit and you forgave everybody who asked. I can't think of a situation where you didn't give a little more than you got.

***

Hi, Mom. Today is Friday, the 2nd of February. I went to the cemetery and it was so cold the tracks near your grave were frozen over and I kept slipping and sliding when I walked to it. It's going to be so much easier to visit your grave in the spring and summer. I look forward to that.

I wish you could tell me what to do about moving. There are a hundred reasons why I should go. You know—all these rational, practical reasons that make sense. There's only one good reason to stay: because this is my home, the home that I grew up in; that you grew old in.

It was a hellhole when Bob was here, but once he was gone we could do whatever we wanted. We could have people over, and go places. I gave you some good years between the time I threw him out, in 1966, and the time I left the *Daily News* and moved to North Adams, in 1977. We had some fun.

When I came home from North Adams in '78 and as I grew older, I spent more time with you and we did eat out a lot, but we didn't go to the Cape anymore; you never saw the ocean again. I should have done better by you.

I was crying the other night, remembering the times when I'd be cleaning you up and you'd lean forward on your walker and say in that little voice, "I'm sorry."

I can't stand the thought that you humbled yourself to me, because I never had to humble myself to you and I never would have had to. You took care of me and supported me and forgave me, and you were always there for me. As crazy as I was, as much trouble as I was, I never had to humble myself to you. But when you got sick and incontinent, you apologized to me—and I let you—and I'm sorry for that. I should have said, "It's nothing, Mother," because it really was. It was cleaning up shit and people do it every day. I wish I had the chance to do it now. I would hope that I would do it with more grace and equanimity.

St. Theresa, the Little Flower, said that sainthood isn't doing something great. It's doing small things with great love. That's how you did things. That's how you made sauce and baked banana bread and corn muffins and tomato-soup cake. That's how you hemmed my clothes, and held my legs when I shook, and fielded my phone calls and proofread my copy and were always my biggest fan.

I know they say you idealize people when they die, but you were, quite simply, the best person I ever knew. I never saw you deliberately hurt another human being. It's not to say you didn't ever hurt anyone, but I never saw you do it on purpose or with malice. When people hurt you, you were always forgiving. All they'd have to do was hold out the olive branch and you were taking it and starting over.

They say the time will come when I can make a life and not think of you every minute. I suppose history would suggest that's true. But I feel split in two, in so much pain that I can scarcely breathe. They tell me I need to take care of myself or I might have a heart attack or get cancer, that grief will do that to a person. But I have to ask myself the question: Do I really want to go on without you? I don't know what the answer is.

Don't worry about me. Don't be sad when you see me suffering. Understand that I have to, because I loved you so and you've been taken from me. I hope we will meet again and then everything will be all right.

***

Hi, Mom. It's Sunday about 9 o'clock. I didn't get to the cemetery today or yesterday but I'll try to get there as soon as I can. Sometimes it's too hard. Sometimes I can't even bear to look at your picture. It makes my heart hurt so much.

You sure went through the mill in those last couple of years. You had such a hard time. You got so frail and your poor little hands got so bruised. Your skin was just falling off you. But still I always felt stronger when I was with you.

You worked so hard and sacrificed so much to leave me this house. I wish we had talked more about the possibility of my leaving it when you died. I think I remember you saying to do what I wanted. I *know* you said I should wait a year. It will be eight or nine months by the time I go, but you were gone from the house for seven months. So, by the time I make the decision to go, it will be a year since you left our home and our home became just a house.

If I go, I hope that you won't be hurt or angry or disappointed that I gave up what you built for us. I don't want to have this house taken from me, although I guess that's what I deserve since I took it from you, or took you from it.

I really was trying to do the right thing for both of us. Although, taking you out on that April 5, and putting you in the car and taking you to Baystate, I knew that I was never going to bring you home.

I wish that there was a way we could have talked about it. But you weren't yourself, and you never would have understood and accepted it. Even if you had, you would have changed your mind an instant later and said, "Let's go home."

Maybe I feel like I don't deserve to live in this house without you. I guess maybe I could have some peace in knowing that I had to give up something, too. I don't know. It's very complicated.

I wish they could put on my tombstone, "Lucy's daughter." That's all I ever wanted to be. "Set me as a seal upon thy heart… love is as strong as death."

I wish you could tell me that all is forgiven and that you're waiting and that we'll be together again. If I knew that, really knew it, it would make everything bearable.

***

It's Monday night, I think it's February 5, I'm not sure. It's 10 o'clock. Annie's in Florida. It's just another reminder that everybody's got a life and I'm no longer the biggest part of anybody's and nobody's the biggest part of mine.

Oh, Lucy. If you had lived to be 100, I would have sat beside you in that nursing home—as hard as it got, as grueling as it got. It was better than this infinite emptiness. My heart is broken. I'm supposed to make a life. I'm not sure how. I'm not sure why.

We had a big snowstorm today, the biggest one in years, I think. At least I don't have to worry about getting you to the hospital if you get sick, or any of that. It's just me now. I just have to get from this lonely, empty night sitting by myself to the moment when I leave this planet.

You'll be there to take my hand—if anything they've taught us is true. And if it's all a crock, then at least I won't be missing you any longer. Maybe all we do is go to sleep and all the pain stops—all the disappointment and longing, the loneliness and regrets, the guilt and sorrow. Maybe we just go away. Even that would be better than this.

You were a good mother and a good friend and I enjoyed our years and our life together. That's why it's so hard for me to leave our home.

I wish I had pulled up my footstool and sat next to you and held your hand when you asked. I figured sitting 5 feet away was good enough, but now I understand how scared you were. Forgive me for all I didn't do. Thank you for everything you did for me, gave to me, were to me.

***

Hi, Mommy. Today is Wednesday, February 6 or 7· It's about 5 o'clock. When I think about things, I realize how much I didn't know about you and I wish that we had talked more. I wish I had asked you a thousand questions about who you were when you were 10 and 20 and when you met Daddy, and I wish I had listened more carefully and had written down everything you said. I guess everybody has those kinds of regrets. First of all, I thought I'd never forget a word you said to me, and of course, I've forgotten so many.

I want to remember as much as I can about how funny you were and how adorable. Gloria was telling Evie the other day that the way Niles got his name was that you urged his mother to name him after *Niles* Standish. That made me laugh; you always had those quirks about names.

I was thinking earlier today about the time that you were in Baystate and they put you in the bed near the window. I would sit in the chair to the left of your bed, facing the TV, and you would doze. That had become my pattern, to sit with you as you slept, wherever you were. That day, I managed to get my hand through the side rails and take your hand. I wasn't feeling well myself, so I wedged a jacket or a pillow against the rail, and rested my head on it.

I remember you woke up kind of abruptly and in that moment you were so clear and so much yourself. You said, in the most loving way imaginable, "How sweet you look." I guess it was a comfort for you to wake up scared and find me there.

It was during that hospitalization that the aide, Renee, who had done a few hours for us at home, had you speak a few words into our answering machine. I came home and found that message: "Goodnight, Pam. I love you." I kept it.

I don't regret making you the center of my life, even though I am so alone without you. Actually, I only regret the time I *didn't* spend by your side. I think what terrifies me isn't so much sitting here alone now, but the prospect of sitting here alone forever.

The snowbanks are so high outside. I don't remember them being so high from one storm since January of '96, when you were in Baystate with pneumonia. It was around the time of my birthday and Annie actually brought my presents to the hospital. When we'd visit you, we'd have to shovel to go out and then when we got home, it would have snowed again so we'd shovel again. We had 18 storms that year as I recall. It was a tough time.

I didn't go to the cemetery for the past two or three days and I feel bad about that. I'll be glad when the weather breaks. It mattered to you that your grave was visited. If it was important to you, then it's important to me.

How hard you struggled against death—until it became impossible to resist any longer. Then you went with great dignity and composure.

I remember your eyes were closed for a long time, a couple of days really. Yet I know, beyond a shadow of a doubt, that in the act of going, you opened them and looked right at me. Your eyes were dark, with a light shining in them. Then you were gone. I remember a note I got from Ruth's friend. She quoted somebody saying, to paraphrase, that "you would take the image of me in your heart to heaven." Maybe that's what you were doing.

***

You were so good to me. I remember when I went to the orthodontist as a kid, I would meet you downtown and we would go to the Waldorf and get egg salad or tuna sandwiches. Sometimes you would say you weren't hungry because you could only afford enough for me. I didn't know that till much later. I would take practically all the pickles in the pickle bowl. You thought that was so funny.

I remember how we took the bus downtown to go to the show, the Bijou or the Paramount, and we would stop at the Mr. Peanut store. You would get a bag of peanuts and I would get popcorn. We would sneak them into the show because you weren't supposed to bring stuff in, but it was cheaper. We had the best times when I was little. I can't express how happy I was to be with you. Waiting for the bus or in the grocery-store line or walking to church, it was all OK as long as we were together.

It hasn't even been three months and it feels as if you've been gone forever. I look down the road and I say, "How can I go on? How can I grow old without you? What will become of me? Will I sit in a nursing home corridor, praying that someone will hold my hand? And who will come for me?" Oh Mom. Will you come for me?

***

Hi, Mom. It's Friday, it's February 9, about 5:30, 6 o'clock. It's been a busy day for me. I had to write something this morning and then I had to deliver it. I met my friend Sally for lunch and then I did a few errands and came home. I don't know why I'm so tired. I know I'm still not eating well. For supper, I had five doughnuts. You'd be thrilled to hear that. I miss cooking for you. There was a reason to get up in the morning and a reason to cook and a reason to do laundry and a reason to keep up the house.

I feel so disinterested in everything. Nothing seems to matter very much. If I'm going to sell the house, why keep it up for the next people? I don't know if I'm doing the right thing or not. Sometimes I think that all of this indecision is you saying to me, "When in doubt, do nothing."

I'm so lonely. I'm not part of anything. I'm kind of odd man out everywhere I go. I'm not essential to anyone. I was essential to you; you're still essential to me.

***

It's Monday morning about 10 o'clock. I think it's the 12th of February and it's very cold today. You would have been so miserable. But you don't have to worry about those things anymore.

***

I watched *Touched by An Angel* on TV last night and I felt like it was a message for me. There was a girl on it, and her name was Lucy. At one point Monica, the angel, said to her, "Do you know what Lucy means? It means 'bringer of light.'" There was a lot of talk about looking at the stars, and, of course, stars were a motif of many cards and expressions of sympathy that I got after you died.

In the TV show they cited that proof for the existence of God that I learned in high school: If you find a watch, you have to believe there was a watchmaker. So there was a lot of synchronicity and it made me feel there was a lesson for me.

I talked to your niece yesterday. I wanted to hear what she had to say because of her connection to you and your life as a young woman.

I sure wish you could smile at me and tell me that you aren't mad at me. That would mean everything to me. I guess those things don't happen every day and maybe you're saving your visit for a time, a week, a month, 10 years, 20 years from now, when my need will be greater. In any case, I hope when it's my turn to go that you'll come for me. Sally says that she's heard and seen that happen many times—a person who is dying will begin talking to someone who has gone before as if that person were right there.

I don't know what I'm going to do about moving. The more I think about it, the more it seems that I need to go. When I become very upset about leaving things behind, I have to remind myself that in the end, they will all go to strangers anyway. I think that the lesson in life is to get attached to nothing. That's easy to say.

***

It's February 14. It's Valentine's Day. I'm watching a Barbra Streisand concert, wishing you were here to watch it with me. I almost know what you'd say: "Boy, what a voice, huh?" But about halfway through, you'd fall asleep. I'd be happy now to have you asleep in the chair.

Nothing's the same without you. I would give most of my life to have you back with me. I would like just enough time to live a little more of it with you.

***

Today is February 18 and I looked at the apartment in Granby again. Evie and I were talking about where to put the cutting boards that you did the tole work on and we found a place. There's a tin cabinet on our back porch. You painted it black and put Amish symbols on the door. We had it for years. I used to keep all my paper supplies in it. I suggested to Evie that we just pull the door off and mount that on the wall. She thought it was a good idea. So that's a big comfort to me, to be able to take that with me.

I was coming down the street the other night and I thought, "Never again will I see my big gray house looming large in the center of the street." But it's not the building that I'll pine for; it's my life with you.

I don't want to become sick and old and have no one.

It's February 19, a Monday. Carmella, your girlhood friend, called you today. "Lucy?" she said. My heart just ached at the sound of your name. You had not heard from her in many years. I told her that you had passed away and she seemed very sad. She said she thought about you all the time. "We were so close and we had so many dreams together. She wanted to be a writer," she said. "I guess that's what you are."

Then she said, "Oh, if I had only called a month earlier!" I didn't say it, but thought, "Oh no, my dear. That would have made no difference."

I've been watching TV since 7 o'clock this morning and now it's 4:30 in the afternoon. I've got about seven hours more and then I'll go to sleep.

I'm anxious to touch base with anybody in the Universe who will talk to me for five minutes and let me mention your name more than once without looking for the exit.

***

It's 7:30. *Hollywood Squares* is on. How you used to love it. "Are the Squares on, honey?" When you were in the nursing home, you asked me once. "Where are the Squares?" I told you they didn't watch that show there. "Oh," you said quietly. "I see." Just one more disappointment, huh?

The day you came out of Woodbridge's and fell and hit your head, both of our lives changed forever. It was a tough six years after that, for both of us. I wonder why we couldn't have had those years to enjoy together. I'm so jealous of everyone whose mother lives to be 90 or 91 or 95. I'm so jealous of anyone who is sitting with her mother tonight.

***

It's February 21, Mom. I have a big project to do. You always had confidence in me and you always gave me a little bit of confidence in myself.

I'm burning a beautiful white taper in front of your picture today. You'd be amazed at how fast I've gone through the candles. You burn one a day, and pretty soon you look and there are no more candles.

I have so much to do if I'm going to move to Connecticut, and it's just hard for me to do anything. I'm kind of immobilized. I get to thinking of you and I just can't seem to do anything else.

I was remembering yesterday how, one time when you were at Baystate, they had the beds facing, instead of side by side. They brought in an elderly woman. Her name was Olive and she was obviously very, very sick—hollow-eyed and hollow-cheeked. You looked at this poor lady and in your sweet way you said, "Hello. If you need anything, tell my daughter and she'll help you." My heart hurt because I knew how bad you felt for her.

A nurse called me out into the hall, and he said, "You should know that this lady is not going to live very long. She's probably going to die within hours … Do you think it will upset your mother?" I said, "No, I'll take care of it."

So I said, "Mommy, that lady's really, really sick and she's probably going to die." You said, "Oh" and you looked over at her so sadly, and I said, "But, you know, she's OK. She doesn't seem to be suffering. Let's say a little prayer for her, OK?" So we did and that seemed to make you feel that you were helping. I closed the curtain so you didn't have to look right at her because I didn't want it to scare you. It kind of scared me. She died within the hour.

You volunteered my services to all your roommates. One night, my friend and I were sitting with you, and the patient in the other bed also had visitors. As they got ready to leave, they asked that woman if she would be all right. "Oh sure," she said. "If I need anything, these fat girls will help me." We didn't know whether to sock her or fall on the floor laughing.

***

I sit in our living-room, Mom, and try to remember all of its incarnations. It was painted a pale green for a while and then a sand color. After we paneled three walls, I remember we painted the other wall, nearest the driveway, blue. You liked that. I don't think you ever really liked the whites and the off-whites as much as I did. It was your home and I should have let you have whatever colors you wanted.

It will be hard to walk out of this house for the last time and leave it to someone else to call home. This was where you and I made our life. I love my memories of Christmases and birthdays here with you, at least those without that screwball to ruin them. Even with the sadness that we bore often and the loneliness that we bore always, we had each other in this place.

I see you in the kitchen most especially. It wasn't so long before you left for the hospital that last time that you had shuffled into the kitchen and tried valiantly to wash the dishes. So when I look into that room I see you.

When I look into the middle room, I picture a dining-room table and a hutch, and milk-glass decorations, and people sitting around talking and laughing.

I look outside and I see the sand that passed for a yard that you gradually transformed. I see the lilac bush that we dug up and moved. I see the stone that you said Daddy put there. I see forsythia, and evergreen trees that stood like little soldiers in front of our porch until you decided that they were rotted and had to come down. You took them down soon after one doctor said you'd be an invalid. They were always wrong about you. I guess that's why I thought you wouldn't die that last time. I thought there was still a chance.

I had them take the procession down the street on the day of your funeral. I hope it doesn't hurt you to be gone from here. It will hurt me to be gone. I will sit alone in a place where you never sat. I will try to remember every corner of this house, every piece of wall, every place your footstep fell. I will listen for the sound of your laughter. I will try to gather up all the memories and take them with me and hope that it will be enough.

I pray that we'll be together, in another place we'll be home.

How do I keep going until I'm that little old lady sitting in the nursing home staring out the window watching for someone who will never come? When I call your name, they won't even know who it is I'm calling for.

I have so many decisions to make about my future and I can't even think straight. I just can't figure out what to do about anything.

***

Hi, Mom, it's Friday, February 22. I went to see your younger brother today. He was in a wheelchair; he's missing a leg due to his diabetes, I guess. He seemed really happy to see me and really sad you were gone. I think in his own way, he did love you. We had a nice little chat. I told him I might move to Connecticut to live with friends and he said, "Don't let them take advantage of you." He sounded like you.

I went to Stop & Shop and I was thinking how much I wished I could get a message from you. There was a truck in front of me at the light that had several bumper and window stickers. On the back window, there was a little one written in script and when I read it, I felt a little jolt. It said, "Fare thee well. We love you more than words can tell." Someone told me later it is a Grateful Dead song, but it felt like a message from you.

***

Today is Friday, February 23. Did a lot of crying today. What's terrifying is to think that you're never coming home. It's not like I'll see you tomorrow or the next day. I'll never see you again. The finality of that is so overwhelming.

I'm so glad that you lived until I was 55. I don't have such a long time to go now. If you had died when I was in my 20s, I couldn't have made it. I couldn't have lived without you to hold me together.

I drive down the street and see our house sitting there in clear view and I think: It's just another house now. I remember that song you used to sing. It was something like, "Lucy doesn't live here anymore..."

And she never will again. Lucy doesn't have my phone number anymore. I don't have to carry the piece of paper with her insurance information on it anymore. We don't have a joint checking account anymore. Lucy is somewhere else. Her body is in the ground at St. Michael's Cemetery and soon there'll be a marker there. Right now there's a tire track across her grave because they had to take a little snow-cat or whatever in there to dig another grave. It broke my heart to see that.

I hope that you are in the arms of a loving God who tells you every day how precious you are in his sight. Because you were precious in mine.

***

It's Saturday, February 24. I went to see Gloria and Evie for a little while and then I went up to see Annie. I did it all today because we're supposed to get freezing rain and ice tomorrow and I'll be afraid to leave the house.

I got home about 9 o'clock. Whenever I see our house, I think, "Behind that window she should be waiting." I should walk in and you should turn, with your eyes sparkling and your face wreathed in that wonderful smile. and say, "There you are. You're home."

So it is tough coming in to an empty house and looking at your little table. It seems like yesterday it held your cranberry juice and your Kleenex. Your oxygen cord was stretched across the floor and your walker was beside your chair. There's so much I want to tell you, to ask you, so much I want your advice about, and you're not here.

Around March I usually start thinking about your birthday and what to do for it. I won't have to give you a party this year. Maybe we can combine your day with a little service for my leaving the house and I can get a cake. Instead of "Happy Birthday, Lucy," I'll have them write "We miss you, Lucy."

***

Today is Monday. It's February 26. I don't think I talked to you yesterday because I was too upset. I felt very separated from you. I didn't light your candle, I didn't go to the cemetery, I tried not to think about you too much. I felt terrible and slept badly and all of that. But today things are different. Not easier necessarily, but different.

***

I'm picking this up on Tuesday, February 27, at about 3:45 in the afternoon. I got interrupted by some phone calls last night and never got back to this. I'd gone to see your priest, Father Jim, and he gave me absolution and Communion and I guess I'm back in the Church if I choose to be. It wouldn't be the first time I've come back and left, so I'm not too optimistic about it.

***

For some reason I was just thinking about how you used to say "normal plus" all the time. I remember everybody in the nursing home, including the doctor, was so perplexed by it. I explained that you used to work as a Kodacolor enlarger and that these terms related to that. From then on, whenever you said "normal plus," he'd smile.

I don't ever want to forget how, months before you died, I'd say to you, "Who's going to take care of me when I'm old, Mommy?" And you'd say, "I'll take care of you, honey." You honestly thought that any day you'd feel better and you'd make macaroni and do the laundry and clean the house and life would be the way it used to be. I think that every time you said, "I want to go home," you were talking about that time, a time when all of those things were possible.

I remember you in the backyard. I would stand in the doorway or on the porch and look down the little hill and you'd be there with a rake or shovel or a little saw, cleaning up your yard. I'd say, "Hi, Mommy." You'd be wearing that bedraggled green jacket, and you would look up and smile your wonderful smile; you were so alive and so full of purpose.

Yesterday I put on that jacket and realized that it has a hood. I never knew until yesterday that it has a hood. Wherever you are now, you don't need a hood—or a jacket.

I picture myself coming up the front walk on a winter day around the holidays and seeing that cheery snowman hanging in the porch window. If things go as planned, that snowman will not be in that window next year—because I won't be here. It makes me very sad to think that our wreath won't be lighting up the porch, but what can I do?

I didn't celebrate Christmas this year. I wonder if I'll be able to celebrate it ever again. It will always break my heart to remember how much you loved it; how like a little girl you were when you opened your presents. When they were all opened, you'd say, "That's all?" I'd say, "Well yeah, Mom." You'd say "Oh, I know you gave me a lot." But still there was that little note of disappointment: "That's all?"

I think there could be 20 people in this room and I'd still be lonely without you. We had 55 years and 10 months together.

***

It's Ash Wednesday, February 28. It's about 8:30 in the morning. Sitting here watching *Today.* I had a little fantasy that you were upstairs washing up, and in a few minutes you'd come downstairs and you'd say, "OK, you ready?"

I see us having lunch somewhere. Maybe on the way home we'd stop and pick up some library books and then we'd come home and have tea or a snack and read or watch TV. At the end of the day you'd turn and say to me, "We had a nice day, didn't we, honey?" I'd say, "Yes, we did Mom. It was a great day."

Instead, I'm sitting here alone surrounded by pictures and memories of you. My heart is aching. Yet how lucky I am. I don't have to be in the work place dealing with people. I didn't have to get up at 6 o'clock and drive up the highway today. The money is not infinite, but if I need to take another month or two or three, I can do that. In the end, as with everything else that I've ever been or had or achieved, I have you to thank.

I marvel at what you were able to do for me; that a woman who walked to work and never was compensated fairly was able to leave her daughter a house, which will either be my home or an investment in my future.

Chapter Ten: Spring

Today is Sunday. I think it's March 1. The people on the news were talking about the Liberty Branch Library. I think we went there every week from the time I was 7 or 8 years old until you were about 70, and then I went alone and got your books for you. Finally, when you got too sick to read, I stopped going—even for myself. I used to read at least seven books a week, all the new fiction. I haven't read a book in three or four years. I hope someday I get back to reading. I know it would be a good escape for me.

I feel like I died with you, Mom. I don't even know who I am anymore.

I went to church and had a terrible anxiety attack. I could barely stay upright. I was afraid I'd pass out. I walk like I have two wooden legs when I'm like that. I'm sure I look peculiar. I can't help it.

***

Hi, Mom, it's Monday morning. I remember how I used to sit at the kitchen table and you would stand at the stove and make me those little silver-dollar pancakes. As fast as you put them on my plate I'd eat them. When I'd finally had enough I would tell you, and then you'd stop and move the griddle to another burner. Then you would clean up the kitchen.

I remember our old Kalamazoo gas stove and the electric stoves after that. I did most of the cooking toward the end, but I remember earlier days: you using the electric mixer, slicing vegetables and peeling potatoes; making big salads and tossing them with your hands the way Grammy used to because it mixes in the dressing better. I remember so many things—all that you did for me.

I remember you going up and down the cellar stairs with baskets of laundry. When I moved the washer upstairs it took up a lot of our kitchen space, but I think you understood that it was better for both of us not to have to go up and down those stairs.

I remember hurrying home from Grammy's on cold nights when I was little, before we converted the furnace, fearing that the coal fire had gone out. I remember you banking and stoking and shoveling coal: such hard, heavy work for a woman. Nothing was easy for you, Luce. I hope you know how much I admire and respect what you did with your life. You started with nothing and somehow made it into something. I started with something and managed to turn it into nothing.

I had such promise at the beginning. Somehow it all fell apart. I tried to reclaim some of it toward the end. I did get another regular column. I think that made you happy. One of the real marks of your losing ground was that you stopped reading what I wrote. I'd read it to you sometimes, but I'm not sure you even got all the jokes any more.

If I have any anger toward God, it's not that He took your body, but that He took your mind. If you had been clear, we could have had those six years. We wouldn't have had to have strangers in our house and life would have been better for us.

***

I have the blue-pink-and-white afghan that Gloria made you. I remember the day when you said, "I'm having trouble cutting this, honey," and I turned and you were trying to cut your afghan in half with little scissors. Within an hour, your mind cleared a little—like the cloud passing in front of the sun. You realized what you had done and you said, "I did a really bad thing. Do you think that Gloria can fix this?" Gloria did.

So you had the afghan with you those last weeks and months at the nursing home. I used to call it your "magic blanket". "Do you want me to go get your magic blanket?" I'd say when you were cold. You'd say "Yeah" and I'd get it and tuck it around you.

What in this house can I bear to part with? The floral footstool cover that you made with no one to help or instruct you? The little straw basket where you kept your sewing things? The blue glass milk jug that we bought at the Cape? The ship? The ginger jar? The rag doll?

How about the little crewel piece you made? It shows a kitten with a ball of yarn. I remember when the woman from church who moved to Florida stopped to see you at the nursing home when she was visiting Massachusetts. "I'm glad I had a chance to say goodbye," she told me. "But your mother didn't know me; she was playing with a ball of yarn." What a change: from doing needlework to rolling up yarn as busy work.

So, what can go then? The gold mirror that you gilded? The little pictures of Grammy and Grandpa? The crucifix that was in your coffin? The Botticelli print? How do I part with any of it Mommy? It's all about you.

***

Today is Friday. It's March 2. I've had a hard day. I try to explain to people that I don't know who I am any more. I was Lucy's daughter. I'm still Lucy's daughter, but Lucy's gone and she doesn't need me any more. What am I here for? What am I supposed to do? I don't know.

I made an appointment with the doctor. I don't know if it will help to see him or if it will just make me cry more. I have so many memories of bringing you to see him.

I'm supposed to have my taxes done Monday and they're talking about a lot of snow that day. If you were here, I'd be telling you how worried I was about driving over there and you'd be worried too. On Monday morning, when I left in the snow, you'd be anxious and when I got home you'd hold out your arms, "Oh, you're all right! I'm so glad, I was so worried!"

I'll never be loved the way I was by you. I miss you. That's all.

Hi, Mom. It's Sunday. I guess it's March 4 and it's about 8:30 in the morning. I woke up with that stomach pain. I had it all day yesterday off and on.

They're talking about this winter storm that's supposed to start tonight and continue until Wednesday, blowing and drifting, blizzard-like conditions. I'm going to be all alone. I'm scared the power or the phone will go out. It would have been so different if you were still alive. I would have gone to the store today and gotten us lots of things to eat and maybe rented a couple of movies. We would have been together, and as long we were together everything was OK.

If you'd been at the nursing home, I guess I would have had to sleep in the lounge. I could not have left you alone for three days.

I'm glad you don't have to be afraid anymore. Please watch over me.

Gloria and Evie wanted me to come down and ride out the storm with them. I felt I had to stay here because I don't want to get dependent on other people. I need to embrace the aloneness and come to terms with it.

You could ask God: Maybe He'll let you come to me in a dream.

***

Well Mom, it's Monday night, almost 10 o'clock and the storm is still going. It looks like we have another 24 hours or so before it ends, and then I'll have to figure out some way to dig out of it.

I remember when that song came out, "Wind Beneath My Wings." I think we actually heard Perry Como sing it the first time and you fell in love with it, and I said "That song makes me think of you, Mommy."

All I want to do is talk about how wonderful you were, and nobody wants to listen; and if they do listen, they don't join in. They don't say, "I remember the time she did that," or "I remember the time she said that." When you are an only child, there is no one to share your history with.

I would give whatever time I have left to spend another evening with you.

***

Hi, Mommy. It's Tuesday. I think it's March 7 or 8. It's about 5 o'clock. It's still snowing from yesterday. Pat next door plowed the driveway apron, and I did the rest. There's still more snow, 3 or 4 more inches, to be shoveled tomorrow.

I'm looking out the window and seeing that it's still light, and realizing that the days are getting so much longer now. You died in November, before the shortest day of the year.

You always said that you weren't as lonely in the winter, that you were content to be at home where you were warm and dry and didn't have to face the elements, and it was dark out and not very inviting. So you said it was OK then to be home alone evenings and weekends.

But in the summer, people are going and doing. They're swimming or having cookouts or going to the park or playing games or riding bikes. They're living in a way that we really never lived. So you would feel more isolated on those long, lush summer days. I guess I feel the same way. I don't know. I'm so used to being lonely now that I don't know any other way to be.

When you left, it's like you turned out all the lights in all the rooms.

***

I remember you ironing for me, pressing that iron into every little crevice of the article of clothing, making it perfect. You did a wonderful job, maybe because you had worked at a laundry when you were younger. You'd hang my shirts and pants up on the molding of the dining room door, and they all smelled so clean and fresh that I couldn't wait to wear everything. Then you would put up the board, reaching up to put the hook in the eye to hold it in place.

Nobody ever worked harder, or tried harder, or gave more and got less in return.

But you had me and I had you. I had a mother who understood me, accepted me, forgave me everything and loved me always. You will live on until the day I die or God strips me of my memory. As long as I remember you, you'll be alive.

***

Hey Mom, it's Wednesday. I have to deal with the snow again. But it's got to be almost the end. It's early March now and spring is coming soon. It breaks my heart that you won't be here for spring. A lot of times during the day I'll say, "I'm sorry you're not here to eat this, Mommy. I'm sorry you're not here to see this." But I guess I don't need to be sorry for you anymore because you're either at peace or in a better place. I guess I'm sorry for me that you're not here to watch the movie and that I won't be making French toast for you tomorrow morning.

So another day goes by, and I'm still alone. I wish that we could have had more time together. At the end of your life, in those last few months, I would say to people "When is she going to die? Is she ever going to die?" That came out of the same kind of rage that once had made us scream at each other, "I hate you!"

I think we yelled at each other because both of our hearts were breaking and we had no one else to yell at. You knew you were going to have to leave me and you didn't want to go. I was so angry that you had to go. So we yelled.

I hate living without you, Mom. Life is so empty, so meaningless. I just have to keep on going. I think you knew that my career was pretty much over, and that I probably was never going to find love. I think that's why you wanted so much to stay with me. Because you knew as long as I had you, I didn't really need anyone else. But you had to go, and now I'm alone.

For all my ranting and raving, and all my complaining, I was content as long as you were with me. I bitched and moaned because that's the way I am. But there were so many times when I would look over at you and think, "Oh God, this is enough. Please let me just have this."

We cried at the same things, laughed at the same things. I'll never have that kind of closeness with another person.

I'm afraid of pain, suffering, suffocating. I'm afraid of being abused or neglected in a nursing home. I'm afraid of all the things around dying. But I'm hoping that when I go, you'll be waiting.

I can picture you saying to God, "Can I just talk to her for a minute?" and God saying, "No, I'm sorry. You can't." And you saying, "See, because she's so nervous." I know wherever you are you're still keeping an eye on me.

***

Hi, Mom, it's Thursday, March 8. I remember when I'd be waiting for the aide to come and I'd be getting really, really nervous. I'd stand looking out the window and you'd stand next to me with your little walker to see if you could spot her first. You were always right by my side, no matter what I was going through.

I know that when I had my gall bladder out, and when I had that little bit of breast surgery, it hurt you that I didn't want you with me. If you only knew how much I wished you could have come with me; you'd always been with me when I was frightened or sick. But the sad truth was that I would have had to be taking care of you while you were trying to take care of me, and then I would have been in worse straits.

So I had Annie come because I needed help. That was a turning point for you, and for me. There were so many places along the way those last few years where I was losing you a little bit at a time: first my advisor; then my parent; then my confidante, and finally, my companion.

I watched you die a minute at a time, a cell at a time. I watched the Lucy I knew and loved—and leaned on, grow older and frailer every minute; and still your spirit shone as brightly. You were still my Mom. It was a hard thing to watch. Most of all it was hard to see the disappointment in your eyes, the frustration, the pain that you couldn't be what you wanted to be anymore. And that agonizing optimism that said, "When do you think I'll start to get better?"

Job said, "Though He slay me, yet will I trust in Him." I guess I can bear what He does to me, but I couldn't bear what He did to you. Maybe someday I'll understand.

I told you when you were dying that I'd be along soon. I said to you, "Time goes by in the blink of an eye in heaven. You'll hardly know that I'm not there, and suddenly I will be." Unfortunately, time goes by more slowly here on earth.

***

Well, it's Thursday the 8th at about 5:30 in the evening, and nobody is free to talk to me. You always listened. I wish I had talked to you more. I found a little note in a journal that you had started, saying, "Pam and I never talk anymore." I thought we did, but I guess I didn't talk to you enough. I have no excuse; no explanation. I know that you were always my favorite person and I loved you best. I always knew that you were the one who truly loved me, and I guess I just figured that you'd be there. But if I had known it hurt you, I would have talked to you more, and I'm sorry that I didn't.

The note is still on the back door that says "Mom, don't go outside, please." I know I should take it down. It has no purpose anymore. But I can't.

That little pencil holder next to your chair—I know there are pencils in it that you used. You would take them out and look at the points and touch them. That's how you judged a pencil. Those pencils are still here, but you're gone.

Everything in this house is about you: the picture of you and me and Brownie; the portrait of you; the picture of you as a little girl with Larry and the goat cart; everything. There's nowhere I can look that I don't see you. I look at that doorway between the dining-room and the living-room and I see you standing there with your walker, looking at me. Sometimes you'd say, "Hi, honey," and I'd say, "Hi, Mommy." I miss the sound of your walker striking the floor.

I would go back and do it all again. I would try to do it better this time, because I'd know what life is like without you.

I don't fit anywhere, Mom. I'm the extra person, the third wheel. You remember that line, 'The Cheese Stands Alone'? I guess I'm the cheese. There's nobody in the passenger seat. There's nobody across from me in the booth. There is only me, and it's as though a piece of my heart is gone.

I was just remembering how I used to sit with you in the nursing home. Sometimes I would hum and sometimes I would sing softly and sometimes you liked me to say the "Our Father." I said to you one night, "Do you want me to sing to you, Mommy? Or do you want me to hum? Or say a prayer?" You looked at me, and thought about it carefully and then you said, "Do a humming prayer." Foiled again!

Got a hang-up call tonight. I wish you were here. As sick as you were, I felt safe when you were home.

***

Hi, Mommy, it's Saturday night, March 10, I guess. I went to visit Evie and Gloria and had dinner with them at a Mexican restaurant. The whole time we were eating, I was watching a baby and I knew that if you had seen that baby it would have made you smile. I knew you would have been fascinated by all the goings-on at the restaurant. I think you would have even liked the food. You never had fajitas. I wish I had introduced you to them.

Evie was talking about her parents' anniversary this fall and having them take a limo ride to a restaurant in Northampton. I found myself wishing that you had ridden in a limo. I don't believe you ever did—except for funerals.

Gloria said there's a star in the sky she calls the Lucy Star. She said it reminds her of you and she never saw it before you died. I saw it. It's a bright one. I don't know what I believe about any of that stuff. I just pray that there is something after this and that you're watching over me and loving me and waiting for me. You always waited for me to come home, so why wouldn't you be waiting now?

So I'm here in our house that's no longer a home, looking at all the things that were yours and wishing you were here with me to enjoy them. We had some fun, Mom. I'm sorry we didn't have more. I'm sorry that time ran out, and I'm sorry that you had so much hurt and sadness before you died.

***

Today is Friday, March 11, and it's pouring rain. For some reason I was thinking of one time when you and I went out to eat at a place on Boston Road. They seated us in a booth in the back. I was in a really bad mood, bitching and complaining, and you were sipping a glass of water. All of a sudden you got this look on your face, this mischievous look, and you spit a mouthful of water across the table and it hit me right in the face. I guess you just wanted me to shut up. We laughed all night. You were so funny.

I long to confide in you and tell you how upset I am and have you make it right for me. I guess that's never going to happen.

***

Hey, Mommy. Today is Tuesday. It's March 21, I guess. I've been crying a lot over the fact that you used to ask me to stay longer at the nursing home and I didn't. Father Jim says that I'm carrying too many regrets. He said, "You've got a lot of baggage. Just let it go. Don't even ask me how. Just let it go."

So I guess that's my job now, to find a way to do that. I remember a friend telling me about a psychic who told her that there's only one fear in life, and that's the fear that God is a lie, and there is nothing beyond this life. If that is the case, then all of this pain is the end of it. That's all we get to have.

I go to church to be connected to you. "Whither thou goest, I will go, and thy people shall be my people, and thy God my God."

I went to the cemetery today. Still snow on your grave. Pretty soon there'll be grass there, and a stone that says "Beloved Mother, Best Friend."

***

Hi. Today is Thursday, the 22nd of March. It's almost midnight. I'm supposed to be working on a project and I don't care about it.

The garage roof has a leak and I don't know what to do. I was hoping that there wouldn't be any big expenses before I move. I'm going to call Ruth in the morning and see if she can come up with any ideas that may be helpful. She's good when it comes to home questions because she has a home.

I feel so alone, and I wish so much that we were together and we were dealing with this as a duo instead of me doing it solo. We were strong together; we were able to get by. Now I'm all alone and I don't know what the hell I'm doing most of the time.

I saw the doctor today. He said all my physical symptoms—the anxiety, the light-headedness, the chest pain, the reflux—are due to grief. Small wonder. I've lost my heart.

Goodnight, Mom. I hope you're having a wonderful time. When I come, you can tell me all about it.

***

Today is Saturday. This is the day we're supposed to move the furniture. I hope there are no catastrophes, nobody gets hurt, and nothing gets broken or damaged. It's a crapshoot in this house because you never know if things are going to fall apart as you're moving them.

I fear sometimes that I'll forget the physical things about you, the little mole on your left cheek, the way the cords of your neck began to stand out because you were working so hard to draw breath; that little cowlick on the back of your head. I've got the same cowlick. We've got the same chin, so many of the same ways. Sometimes when I laugh, I hear you laughing.

I'm sorry you couldn't have lived in a perfect place where everything would have been nice for you. God, for months you slept in a chair, and never complained. I was glad we were finally able to fit that little bed in the middle room. At least you got to stretch out sometimes. Maybe it wasn't what you wanted, but it was something. Kind of the story of your life: never what you wanted, but something.

I hope it was better than nothing. I hope life with me was more good than bad for you. You gave me everything.

I miss our ways, our routines and rituals. I look into the kitchen and see you at the kitchen sink, cleaning off the kitchen table, sweeping the floor, doing laundry. I see you having to lean in to pull the clothes out of the washer, because you were so short, and then hanging them on the rack, folding them up when they were dry. I see you making me a cup of tea, carrying it in so carefully so it wouldn't spill. I hear your voice from the bottom of the stairs. "Pamela, time to get up, little sweetheart."

I don't know how much life I have left, but I would gladly give up all but one day of it to have you back in your chair today. I know that you're better off—even if all you're doing is sleeping forever. No more waiting for the calls that don't come, no more wondering why your family didn't love you more, why your husband left you. No more struggling for air. No more pain or suffering. You're free of it all now.

I hope that if I get to you someday, you'll be glad to see me. I'll sure be glad to see you.

It's 10 o'clock at night. Gloria and Evie and Randy helped me today. We moved out your beautiful dresser. I remember the time a friend from the Marine Corps burned the top of that dresser with a cigarette. I don't think I supported you enough about that. I made light of it because I didn't want a confrontation. I'm sorry. I love that dresser, too. Ruth said she would buy it.

I'll miss my own dresser as well, because you bought it for me and it almost matched my twin bed. I think I've had it since I was 12 years old.

We moved out the nightstand that Bob used—I was glad to get rid of it. We moved your sewing machine—you were so disappointed when it stopped working. The cedar-lined wardrobe chest is gone; I think 50 cats climbed up the side of that chest to sit on top of it. It was badly scratched but we never had one single thing eaten by a moth except the stuff we didn't put in that chest. I had to let it go for a song. We also put out a twin-bed frame, the filing cabinet from down cellar and tons of small stuff.

I'm hoping to make about $500 on the tag sale. I think that when I get over the sadness about seeing all those things go, I'll be relieved because I won't have to worry about them anymore. As I pare things down, I think I'll feel a little more comfortable about moving.

It's hard doing this without you. It's like my heart is on automatic pilot and I just do what I have to do. I empty your bureau. I go through your things. I throw things away, give them away. I don't know where the strength is coming from.

I look down the road and all I see is more loss and more sadness and it's hard to have any zest for life when there's so much loss.

I pile my papers in your chair now. I hope that's not disrespectful to you. It's just that I can't bear to see it empty.

When I was going through things in the garage the other day, I found a tiny metal star. I like to think that you sent it to me, letting me know that I'm doing a good job and that you're proud of me. I hope you are. I know I didn't make of my life everything that you had hoped I would. I know that in some ways I was a disappointment to you. But I loved you. It was such a comfort to have someone I loved so much who loved me just as much in return, who always cared about me, who was so loving and so generous.

***

Hi, Mom. Today is March 27 or something. I was just looking at some tomatoes I bought and remembering how you planted tomatoes—one time at the side of the house and one time behind the garage. I guess we never did much of a garden. I wish I had helped you more with that. I wasn't into the yard work too much. But you did everything or tried to do everything. You tried knitting and crocheting and gardening and sewing and tole painting. And you were a hell of a good baker.

I often think what a pretty home you made for us, Lucy. You dressed up this old house and made it look better than it deserved to look. I'm sorry I can't stay here and continue that for you. If I were younger, I would.

I will remember as much of it as I can, and I will carry it in my heart wherever I go. It hurts me to leave this place where we built our life but I don't see that I have a choice.

***

Hi, Mom. Today is Wednesday. I remember, toward the end of your time at home it was so hard for you to walk to the bathroom. You'd use the handle that Evie installed to lower yourself and pull yourself up again. I don't know where you found the will. It came from someplace deep in you I guess.

I think somebody once wrote a poem or a song called "My Mother's Hands." I can understand why, because I miss seeing your hands. They became frail as you got older. You'd get those terrible black-and-blues all over them and they shook from all the drugs. You also had that little bump on your left forefinger from arthritis.

You'd say so sadly, "Look at my hands." You could have been complaining pretty much every minute of the 10 years that ended your life. But you were strong and you were kind and as long as you recognized me, you always put me first.

I wish you were here with me. I wish we were talking. I wish I had quit my job sooner, tried to build my freelance business. I could have just pared down some things and we wouldn't have needed as much home care. I think it would have worked out.

I wish we had spent the last year that you were home together. We're coming up on April 5, the anniversary of the day I took you out of this house knowing in my heart that I was never going to bring you home. I live with that sadness every day of my life. Sometimes I think I'll never be able to forgive myself for it.

I have been blessed all my life with total recall, with a wonderful memory. I think that God will take that from me before I die. I believe that what we love most is taken from us before we go. So if our physical strength was important, we become infirm, and if our mental strength was important, we lose our ability to reason, and if we could play the piano, we won't be able to at the end. I just have that sense of the universe not being a very kind place.

Anyway, I find myself remembering things that cause me such pain that sometimes I burst into tears. I remember you in that Geri-chair looking at me with your big eyes, struggling to get a breath into those poor tired lungs. You'd arch your back a little and try to get up. You thought if you could get up, you could get to a place where there was air.

I didn't know what to do, Mom. I fought for you as best I could. I demanded more medicine. I gave you a bolus of morphine from the pump when I had the power to do it. I made them increase the dose when what they were giving you didn't seem to be working. That did seem to give you some relief toward the end; at least it would make you sleep. And when you slept, you didn't struggle.

I sat beside you as much as I could. I thought if I could ease your terror, it would all be easier for you, and I think it was. But I wish that I had come an hour earlier and stayed an hour later. I wish I could have done more and done it better.

I see you in that striped shirt with the white collar, your purple pants and white sneakers. You would be running your hands through your hair and staring at a spot in front of you. Then somebody would say, "Look who's here, Lucy."

You would turn, and your face would light up and you'd say, "There you are," and hold out your arms and make a little noise of contentment as you hugged me and patted my face. Sometimes you'd put a soft kiss on my cheek and kiss my hands. "Sit down, honey. Sit with me." I would give anything to be back there now.

People ask me if it's a relief to have you gone. Jesus, no. No relief, Luce. I'm sorry I ever complained. I will never forgive myself for saying to friends, "Is she ever going to die?" with the kind of sarcasm that suggested I was such the victim. I wish I had never said those words. I was overwhelmed, I guess, and it was my way of venting. But I'll never forgive myself.

The truth was that sitting beside you gave my life meaning. I had a purpose when I got up in the morning and now, truly, I have none. I have tasks, I have things that I must do, but no purpose, and I don't know that I'll ever find it without you.

My goal is to be with you again, and to do whatever it takes to make that happen. If that means wearing sackcloth and ashes, or walking on my knees up the Via Dolorosa, I would do that. Basically I would do anything if I knew that at the end of the road you would be waiting.

So that's my goal. But I don't think that you could call it a purpose. I am a motherless child with nobody to make happy. Annie would say, "You have yourself." I don't know how to communicate to anyone how empty that is.

***

Hi, Mom. Today is Monday. It's the 2nd of April. I haven't talked to you in a little while. Sometimes it just hurts too much. Tonight's one of those nights when I feel you in the room, and feel the absence of you at the same time. I miss you desperately.

April 5 is coming, and I'm in so much pain. I think in some ways, it's a sadder day than the day you died. I couldn't do anything about your dying, but after they "butterflied" your finger that day, I could have found a way to bring you home.

All I can tell you is what I've said a thousand times before: If all of your problems had been physical, I would have cared for you myself. It would have been easy, because you could have cooperated with me. You would have known that you were in your home and that I was Pam, and we could have done it together as we had done everything else together. We were a pretty good team. But I didn't know what to do because you got so mixed up.

I am so sorry.

***

Today is Sunday. It's April 8, the day after the tag sale. I sold almost everything, and made almost $300. I had to let a lot of things go for next to nothing, but I felt that I wanted to part with the stuff now—on my terms.

Until the day I die, I'll regret that you never got a chance to say goodbye to your home and the things you loved. But maybe it would have been too heart-wrenching. Maybe it was better to maintain the fiction that someday you would come home. You could hang on to that glimmer of hope. I tried to keep that alive for you without giving you too much. It was a hard line to walk.

Sometimes in the old days, when we would fight, you would say to me, "You don't understand me at all." It was and is like a knife in my heart. It is true that you were a complicated woman. You had a difficult life. I can't even imagine what it must have been like to have Daddy walk out on you and never look back; how that must have hurt you. Then to marry that nutcase and be pushed around by him: awful. You had a lot of struggles. Yet you tried so hard to stay optimistic and positive. Voltaire said to "tend your garden," and you were the embodiment of that philosophy. You left your little corner of the world better.

I keep going over the words on that postcard I found in my box of Marine Corps memorabilia. It didn't belong there. It was a postcard you sent me when you went on your one-and-only cruise, five years after I got out. It was dated July 1974, but looked brand-new. I showed it to someone because I was so touched by it. When she read it, she said, "Have you considered the possibility that this is a message for now?"

The card said "Dear Pam, I enjoyed every minute. I didn't get seasick. Miss you. Something doing every minute. Don't worry about me. Love, Mom. P.S. You're a good daughter." This woman read that message to mean: "I *enjoyed every minute* of our life together and you don't have to be sad or sorry about any of it. We had a wonderful time. *I didn't get seasick* crossing over. It was easy going from this world to the next. *Miss you.* Even though I'm happy now, I still miss you and love you. *Something doing every minute.* I'm having a good time here. I'm happy. *Don't worry about me.* Everything is OK for me. I'm safe. Love, Mom." And then that little postscript that was so out of place on a vacation postcard *"You're a good daughter"* with three exclamation points—because you know I'm suffering about that.

So who's to say? It is a comfort to imagine you telling me those things now.

It hurts me to know that you don't need me anymore. That's hard because the model that you set for me was when you love, you serve. But now there's nothing I can do but visit the cemetery once in a while and light a candle in front of your picture and talk to you. I wish you were here to help me figure it out.

I'm planning to go to church today. I'll pray that you will help me find my way home to you. Put a light in the window, like you always did for me.

***

Hi. It's about 9 o'clock on Sunday, April 2. I find myself dozing off the way you used to do. I'm aging faster than you did. I think that's because, first of all, you had so much more energy to begin with, and secondly, because you had so much enthusiasm for life right up until you got desperately sick. I respected that because certainly, on the face of it, you didn't have all that much reason to be enthusiastic.

I found a big legal folder with your directions for tole painting; I keep finding a lot of your crafts and notes on how to do things. I hold things that you bought and treasured, and I think how very much you valued beauty. I'm sorry the house became so crowded and disarrayed at the end. We wanted to keep you home and just didn't have enough space for all the medical stuff and everything.

In my mind and heart I'll carry a picture of the way things used to be when I was at the *Daily News* and we were entertaining all the time. The house rang with laughter then. All the leaves would be in the dining-room table; it would be opened up with the lazy Susan on it. We'd sit in the ladder-back chairs. Maybe we'd have to bring an extra chair in from the kitchen.

We'd go into the living-room later, and all your bottles were in the windows. It was a pretty little house. I remember how you did your painting and made your flowers and tried needlework and put plants in the front yard and tried so hard to keep everything looking nice. I marveled at your zest for life despite always having gotten short shrift. I guess that's why you were my hero.

***

Hi, Mom, today is Tuesday, it's April 10. I've been very busy working. It's kind of hard and yet it's good not to think as much. Every time I stop doing, I find myself devastated by the absence of you. I don't know how to explain how much I miss you. It's like somebody cut me in half and now I'm trying to live with half of everything.

I know the last few months and weeks of your life were very, very hard for you. You're better off. I don't question that. But I'm not better off, Mom. There are some nice times, but there's no joy. I just want to see you again. Truly, you are the light at the end of the tunnel for me.

At least when I talk into this tape recorder, nobody changes the subject.

***

Today is Wednesday. I think it's April 11 and it's quite late. I wanted to get into this tape two memories. One of them came from a conversation I had with your niece. She told me that not a day goes by that she doesn't think about you.

She said that the other day she found a doily she had made, and she started to cry because she remembered that she had tried to follow the instructions and the thing was supposed to be nine inches in circumference or in diameter, or whatever. Anyway, she said by the time she finished it, it was about 4 feet wide. She brought it over here and laid it on our living-room floor and she said that you laughed and laughed. I could just see you rocking back and forth, with your face wreathed in laughter. I love that story.

The other memory was how I used to try so hard to give you a wonderful Christmas—when we were alone and we could have nice Christmases. I remember the first year that I was in the Marine Corps. I was making money and I was coming home for Christmas. So I bought you everything I could think of, including a pretty little ring. Jewelry was inexpensive at the Base Exchange. We had a wonderful Christmas that year.

On another Christmas after Bob was gone, I bought you one of those bed pillows that had little arms to support your elbows so you could hold a book. It was brown corduroy. I was so pleased with myself. You opened it and started laughing, and then you gave me a present. I opened it and it was the identical pillow. So for some time, we both had these big honking corduroy pillows on our beds. I think they both eventually ended up in the attic and then we sold them at a tag sale. I wish I had one now.

I've been wrestling again with whether to sell the house and go live in Granby. I was crying because you didn't want to leave this house either. So if I have to leave it, maybe that's only fair.

I hope that finally you're in a place where you feel truly loved. I hope that every once in a while you look down on me and smile.

***

Hi, Mommy. It's April 12, Holy Thursday. It's 7:30 at night and I've been awfully sad all day. This is the 20th week that you've been gone and it feels like you died yesterday. My heart is so raw. I would like to be at the nursing home, with you dozing in the chair and me holding your hand and singing "Scarlet Ribbons" or "My Buddy" and comforting you the way you comforted me all my life. This world is not a very happy or friendly place for me now.

I get through the days the best I can. Right now my job is to get the house emptied out so that, whether I go to Connecticut or stay here or get an apartment, I won't have so much stuff to deal with. It's hard to let go of the things that surrounded us. I've got to get the rest of the stuff out of the attic. I've got to get the stuff that I want to take with me into one place, and I've got to go through your jewelry and more papers and all of the Christmas ornaments. Those will be hard.

I have that audiotape of you trimming a tree so many years ago and I can hear you say on the tape, "I'm trying to pick the red ones because I know you like those best." It will be hard to get rid of the red ones.

I don't think I'll ever have a tree again. So I'll go through all of those things and I'll get rid of what I can and keep what I can't bear to discard. I'll have another tag sale in July.

I should be grateful for the gift of life and every new day. I try, but my heart is empty and my days are empty and my house is empty. I don't want you to be sad. I want you to be happy. You've earned your happiness. You just need to understand that I can't get over you in a few weeks or months. It's as if someone took my heart out.

You turned to me once; it was a year, a year and a half ago. You gave me your sweet smile and you said, "You'll be all right, honey." I guess in a way I am all right. I do my work and I pay my bills and put out the trash and do what I have to do. But I long to be reunited with you.

I thank God that you lived until I was 55 years and 10 months old because no matter how you slice it, I'm in the home stretch.

***

Hi, Mommy. It's Holy Saturday, April 14, and my heart is breaking. I remember last Easter. You were either in the nursing home or the hospital, I can't remember which, but I ate at Friendly's and spent the day alone, except for visiting you. I realized then how very much alone I would always be.

I went to church last night for Good Friday. It was very moving. I wish that I had taken you to more services toward the end of your life. I wish I had brought you to the Dominican Monastery. I wanted that to be just for me. Now I know how incredibly selfish I was. It was quiet there and peaceful, and I could have wheeled you right up the ramp and into the chapel and we could have listened to the nuns chant. Maybe you would have fallen asleep. I think you would have liked it. But I was into my "I deserve something" phase and I didn't want to take you. I was afraid if I took you once, you'd always want to go and there would be another thing I didn't get to do for myself.

Let me tell you, Mom, this doing for yourself thing is vastly overrated. I'm sitting here now. I've got a house, I've got a car. I could go see a Broadway show, book a trip to Europe, take a cruise like the one you took. There's nothing I couldn't do if I really wanted to do it. And there's not a goddamned thing that I want to do,

I hope you're getting everything you deserved. I hope you are in a place of light and peace and joy. I hope that you're not worried about me.

***

Hi, Mommy. It's Easter Monday, April 16, 2001, about 10 o'clock at night. I miss you. I went to the cemetery yesterday and I didn't bring you any flowers because I wanted to check out the lay of the land, as you used to say. I want to rake your grave up a little bit and put a flower on it, but it's supposed to rain tomorrow so I might not get there until Wednesday or Thursday. I will go, Mommy, and I will remember you for the rest of my life.

You know, I come home every day and invariably I weep because you're not here and I feel as if nobody really understands. But that's how it always was with us. That's why we were so close, because you understood me and I understood you, although not as well, I admit. I wasn't as understanding as you were. But we had each other, and somehow that was the compensation in this life for all the things we didn't have.

You used to quote that line, "Home is where, when you go there, they have to take you in." I guess I don't have a home like that anymore. And so I wait. I long for the day when I pass through that tunnel. I'll be scared and then I'll see your face and my heart will nearly explode with joy and everything will be OK.

I'm trying to find the courage to go on and make something of the time I have left, to make it count, to "work out my salvation," as the nuns used to say. I'm trying hard, Mom. But I'm so sad. My sadness gets deeper every day, I think. It's supposed to get better, but here I am, going on the sixth month, and it's just as hard as the sixth week and the sixth day and the sixth hour.

I'll make your grave pretty as soon as I can. I know you understand. "Mothers forgive everything," you said.

***

Today is Thursday, April 18 or 19, or whatever it is, and Thursdays are always harder for me. I was thinking about the absurd things that I'm grateful for sometimes. For instance, I'm glad you were never the victim of a crime. I remember you said you were walking out the side door at Standard Photo one day and a young boy was standing there, and you said he looked a little fishy, like he was about to grab your purse or something. You looked him full in the face and smiled and said, "Hello, son." And he just stepped back and let you pass.

There was another time you came out and found that someone had popped your ignition. That could have been a lot worse; they could have stolen the car and you would have been devastated by that. You had the car towed and they fixed the ignition and I think we bought one of those steering-wheel locks and all was well.

So there were some heartaches that you were spared in life. God knows you had your share, but you were spared some.

I use your shower now because I had the tile upstairs grouted. I don't think there's been a day yet that I haven't cried while I'm in there. I'm struck by how cold it is when I first step in. I remember how you used to say, "Ooh, it's cold." And I, in my usual charming fashion, would say, "It's not cold. I've got the hot water on. It's steaming hot for Christ's sake! How can you be cold?" I stand in there and I weep because you *were* cold, honey, and I didn't know.

I was so quick to dismiss what you said. I thought I knew so much about everything. I was the expert on the world, and you were just Lucy.

The truth is that I'll never measure up to the person you were. I'll never be as tough. I'll never be as brave, as capable, as wise, as stoic, or as just plain decent as you were.

There were a million things I wanted to do at your funeral, you know? I wanted to have that song "You and Me Against the World" and the poem "Lucy," but if I had had a funeral that went on for 20 hours with a cast of thousands, I couldn't have said all that there was to say about you or how much I love you.

I wake up in the morning and my first words are "Hello, Mommy. I miss you." I go to bed at night and my last words are "I love you, Mommy. I miss you."

I'm still undecided about the move. Gloria and Evie stopped by last night and I wanted them to see how much I had done in the cellar and the attic so that they'd know how hard I was working.

I think I should go. I think it's almost a spiritual exercise, this letting go. I'm too attached to my house and my street. Everything just holds me and maybe I need to start letting go of the things that I love. I tell myself that even when I go, I'll have some money in the bank and if it doesn't work out, I'll have options.

Father Jim says that those we love who have gone before us have an intercessory role. If it is true, then ask God to bless me and show me the way.

***

Today is the 22nd of April. It's about 7:30 in the morning. I'm going to the 8 o'clock Mass and then I'm going down to see Gloria and Evie. I just wanted to tell you that I'm thinking about you today. It's been 21 weeks since you died. I miss you very much. In some ways it's as though it were yesterday. Sometimes the wound is so raw that I can hardly bear it.

I wish I were making you French toast. I still can't eat it. I decided today that on your one-year anniversary, I'll eat French toast. It will be my way of remembering what it was like with you.

I talked to a friend from the Marine Corps. I told her I was all screwed up and that I wasn't getting anywhere, and she said that she thought that I was accomplishing a lot. She said, "You know it's hard to do it alone, without somebody to bounce it off of, without somebody to say, look at this, remember this?" She said, "I think it's very, very hard and I really feel for what you're going through."

I go through it alone, and I weep and I talk to you. In the end, we had each other. That was the law of compensation that my favorite teacher, Sister James Mary, used to talk about.

Anyway, it's kind of a gray morning but it's supposed to get up to about 80 today. Way too hot for my taste. I haven't been out to your grave for a few days, not since I brought the carnation. I'm sure it's long gone. I need to get into more of a routine about when I visit you. I'll try to get better about bringing you flowers during the good weather.

I'll be glad when they put your stone in, Mommy. Then I can bring a little brush and brush it off. Something I can do for you.

I'm sure there'll be work for me this week. And so life goes on. I've been called to jury duty. I'm praying that I don't have to serve. I just don't have the heart for it. I'm afraid if I am picked, I'll just sit there and cry.

***

Hi, Lucy. Today is Monday, April 23. I was thinking today about that bedspread you bought for me when I was young. It was box-tailored, white cotton and had tiny yellow flowers with green stems. I think I either gave it away or put it out at a tag sale some years ago, and now I'm wishing I had it back because you bought it for me. I hope whoever got it after me liked it as much as I did. It was so pretty, so bright and airy. You always liked things to be bright and cheerful. That's how I'll always think of you.

I had a bad day yesterday and a tough night. I hope that you still remember me. I hope that you'll be there to greet me when I come. I made a little shrine for you today. I'm sure everyone will make fun of it, and I could really give a rat's ass because I like it. It has a picture of you when you were in your early 30s. You had clipped a little poem from a magazine—"To My Child," by Ann Campbell, and inserted it into the frame. It goes: "You are the trip I did not take. You are the pearls I cannot buy. You are my Italian lake. You are my piece of foreign sky."

I put that picture on the hutch with several others, including one of us together when I was about 4.

Oh Mom, I look at the picture of you when you were 3, and it breaks my heart. I wish I could have been your friend when you were 3 and 5 and 10. I remember you used to say to me when we'd be talking, "Remember when we were small?" I'd say, "No Mom. I wasn't small with you. I'm your daughter." And you'd say, "Oh, that's right" and we would laugh. It was as if we'd always been together.

I think of that Wordsworth poem, "She lived alone and few could know when Lucy ceased to be. But she is in her grave and oh, the difference to me."

I wonder where you are. Are you in the sky? Or are you in a separate but parallel universe? Are you standing right next to me but I can't reach into that dimension? I pray that you're not just dead. I can't believe that all that love, all that magic just went away. Father Jim says it doesn't make sense that our poor broken bodies remain and that everything that makes us truly wonderful disappears. I want to believe he's right.

I went through a lot of cards and letters tonight—your cards to me, all picked out with such love, such care, with your notes: "Dearest Pam, you are so marvelous. ... The best daughter I ever had."

Please ask God to have mercy, to make some of this pain lift. I can't bear it.

***

Hello Mama. Today is April 29. It's a Sunday. Tomorrow is the last day of April and then we begin the month of May, which used to be my favorite month because it was pretty and it was your birthday month. You could see all your plants budding in the yard and you were so happy to watch the flowers come up.

It's a beautiful month but this year it will be bittersweet. There's no joy in much of anything these days. The deadline looms and I'm still wrestling with the decision about whether to move to Granby.

I've called a real estate agent. I'd like to know what she thinks about the house.

You went through so much. You lost both of your parents in two weeks. You had two lousy marriages. You lost friends. You had your heart broken. Yet you were able to love life and cling to it. You loved books and movies, nice meals, the ocean and the mountains. Every thing I gave you and every place I took you was a joy to you. I wish I had your spirit.

I love our home. I don't think the yard has ever looked prettier. But I just don't know if I can keep this up all by myself.

Am I moving too soon? Am I doing this too fast? I'll be here for three more months, but once I commit to rent the apartment, I really can't renege.

I hate having to move to Connecticut. If I just moved within Springfield, to a little apartment, I'd have less hassle. I don't know. Time's run out now. I either have to say yes or no tomorrow night.

Sometimes I hear you saying, "Go with them. You can't be alone, honey." But I don't know. Maybe you'd say, "Stay in your house. Live in one room. At least it's yours." Please help me.

***

Today is Friday. I think it's the 4th of May. Next week at this time I'll be planning your little party. Stupid, I know, because you're not here, but in my heart you will be. It's a house blessing but it's also a celebration of you and your life.

I've been sick since Wednesday night. I had jury duty yesterday. I prayed really hard I wouldn't have to serve, and I think you interceded for me on that one. My stomach's awful bad. I have a lot of pain and nausea and I'm not doing too well.

I wish we could turn back time, or that this had been a dream and that we could start over again. I would do it better this time.

But your body is in a hole at St. Michael's and I hope your soul is in heaven. I can't do anything for you now except to tell you, over and over again, that I'm so sorry.

***

It's Saturday, May 5. I've been really sick. I'm so sorry for all the times I yelled at you when you were sick. I really was devastated, you know, and my way of coping was to get angry.

I was just going through your little jewelry box from the Bahamas. You loved that cruise so much. I'm looking at the ring that I bought for you 35 years ago at Parris Island when I was in Admin school. You didn't wear it all that much, not like your pinky ring that you wore all the time. But you kept it in a little jewelry box by your side.

One night you said, "I've tried so hard to get better and I'm never going to get better." It was so sad. Your mind got confused. Sometimes you wanted your Mama and your Papa. But at other times you knew exactly what was going on. You'd touch my face and say, "Oh, my poor baby."

What would you say to me now, Mom? I'm so sick. I can't eat. I don't know if it's physical or emotional. Maybe it's the loss of the house. I don't want to go. I know if I don't go everyone will be mad at me. But I still don't want to go. I don't want to leave you behind.

I like the sign on the porch that you painted because it says 'Hello' and I can hear you saying it. You were full of enthusiasm for life. You were always hoping that tomorrow would be better.

***

Today is May 11, the 85th anniversary of your birth.

You came to this house when you were 23, full of hope and love. Daddy told you he would buy you a better house when he "got on his feet." But he never did. In fact, a decade later he was gone, leaving you mired in debt and disappointment. Everyone told you to sell the house—everyone except your father. You said he told you, "If you have a roof, you can always eat bread."

So you got a job, wrote to the bank, began paying off Daddy's debt, then the mortgage. You put in a new sink, and fenced the yard and sewed curtains with ball fringe. When you were done with your 40-hour job and the "woman's work"—keeping a house and making a home, you turned to man's work. You stoked the coal fire, patched, painted, shoveled and mowed.

In your world, you came third. I came first, then our home, then you. So I got braces and the house got circuit breakers while you wore the same coat for 10 years. To you, love was always a verb.

You remarried when I was 13 and you were 41. You thought the marriage would make life better. It didn't. He abused us both mentally, emotionally and verbally. We feared him and he won most fights. But there was one he never won. "Put my name on this house," he would demand. "No," you would say, finding the strength somewhere to resist. "It's my house. I worked to keep it. It's mine and my kid's."

When, at age 21, I booted him out of our lives, we were emotionally spent and burdened by the debts he had incurred, but we still had the house.

Four months later, I headed for active duty. I remember you standing at the storm door, waving—barely able to stand, I suspect, beneath the weight of your sorrow. I wrote and called and came home often, and the three years passed.

Within a week of my return, you were hospitalized for surgery. Sitting here late one night, I realized how empty the house was and I understood how hard the three years must have been for you. I wrote something on a sheet of paper I still have. I wrote, "I will never leave you so alone again." I never did.

We had a good life in this house. We had sweet days and quiet nights, a lot of good food, much laughter, a few good friends. There were heartbreaks, but we endured. We still had our home and each other. Then you began to suffer setbacks physically. In the beginning you were able to bounce back quickly. But from June of 1994 until you left me in 2000, there were countless hospitalizations and only one request," I want to go home."

I heard you, Mommy. I brought you home, when the doctors said I couldn't and the nurses said I shouldn't. I brought you home every time except the last. I'm sorry for that. I wish I could have defied them one more time. But you were so fragile and I was so tired.

You left home on April 5, 2000. It's still our house but the heart of it is gone. So I am thinking it is time to move on. I don't want to. I love our living-room where we read and talked and opened Christmas gifts and comforted each other with cups of hot tea. I love the old-fashioned kitchen. I love the yard where you planted scrub pines and watched them grow to brush the roofline. I'll miss the lilac bush, the azalea bushes and your irises.

I love the front porch where we watched the cars—and the stars. I'll miss the bedroom where you read yourself to sleep, and the hall where you would pause to say goodnight.

I may live in other places, but when I speak of home, I will mean this house and wherever you are now.

***

It's Saturday, May 12, the day after your birthday. Gloria and I went to your memorial Mass and to the cemetery. Gloria had brought some lilacs from Granby and we put them on your grave. I'm sure they were dead a minute later, but they looked pretty. Then I got ready for the house blessing. The minister and her partner, who is a nurse, Annie, Gloria, Evie and Ellie were here.

People brought flowers for your birthday—peonies, a calla lily, a rose and bleeding hearts and lilacs. I got a cake. We sang "Happy Birthday," just as if you were here.

A part of the event consisted of people giving me little gifts to wish me well in my life without you. One friend sent a sign. It is yellow and lavender with a star, and she had inscribed the William Wordsworth poem, "Lucy." The line that I had forgotten from that poem struck me: "As fair as a star when only one is shining in the sky."

The nurse said I was thought of at the nursing home as being a "model of devotion." That meant a lot to me. One of the aides wrote to me after you died, "She must have been one special lady." Well, you were.

I think the surprise of the night for me was a card from Jan. She was the last person to love you, and your last act on this earth was to lift yourself off the bed when you saw her. She told me that she understood how I must miss you and she thought of you often. She said when she has a bad day she looks at the picture that I gave her of the two of you and it gives her some encouragement. I'm so glad.

I tried to make them see last night how special the connection was between you and me. I remember that letter you wrote to me when I was in the Marine Corps about a friend who had taken you out. "She's not you, Pam. She doesn't laugh at the same things we do." Nobody laughs at the same things, Mommy. Nobody cries at the same things either.

This morning I tried to clean out your pocketbook and in the end I put everything back just as it was. Your pocketbook was your constant companion until you got to the nursing home. "Where's my pocketbook, honey? Bring me my pocketbook, honey. Oh my God, I can't find my pocketbook!" That was something else you had to give up when you left home.

I hope that when you got to heaven you found everything exactly the way you wanted it.

I'm supposed to talk to a psychic next week. I used to have more hope in those people than I do now. Now I kind of start from the position that they're full of crap and will only say something to upset me. If she tells me you've already been reincarnated and you're living in Italy, or something, it will just send me over the edge.

I wish the phone would ring and you'd say, "Pam? It's me, Mommy. I miss you like hell." I'd say, "I miss you. too, Mom. But I'll be home before you know it."

***

Hi, Mom. It's Sunday, May 13. It is my first Mother's Day without my mother and it was hard. I didn't go to the cemetery, and I feel bad about that. I went Friday and Saturday, and I'll try to go tomorrow. I hope you understand.

I went to church today and Father wished all the mothers a happy Mother's Day. He said that for those of us who have lost our mothers, it's very hard, but we need to remind ourselves that for them, "Now is the glory."

I hope you had a happy day wherever you are.

I enjoyed every minute I spent with you. I think in this life we have one person, maybe if we're lucky, who really loves us. I had you.

I'll be 57 years old on my next birthday. I hope that if I live a long time and I get really old that you'll still know me when you see me; that you'll see the old lady that I've become and say, "Oh, that's my Pam."

Chapter Eleven: Hard Choices

Today is Monday, May 21. It's been more than a week since I last spoke into this recorder. I think that is because a week ago today, on the 14th of May, I signed the papers and we put the 'For Sale' sign in front of the house. It was too hard to talk about.

It's been up a week and we've had three or four people go through. One couple stayed for 45 minutes and I was hoping they were going to make an offer, but they didn't.

I found out that a guy next door, who's said to be a felon, knows that I'm alone here, so I'm very nervous that he's going to break in. It makes me realize there are too many reasons why I can't stay here alone. I thought about just putting in an alarm system and hanging in here for another couple of years. But I'm kind of scared to stay here without you, and there's so much maintenance that needs to be done and my income is so limited now.

So I'm doing the best I can.

***

Today is May 24. It's a Thursday. I actually invited myself down to Granby today and had dinner with them because I was so lonely.

A lot of people have come through our house. I know you would hate that. They've walked through and poked around and now they're all gone. We've got three more scheduled tomorrow, and then I'm sure we'll have them over the weekend. So it's starting to get to me in a big way.

I don't know if they're seeing something they hate, or the price is too high, or what. I'm kind of sorry I went with this particular Realtor but I signed a goddamned contract.

I think it's such a nice house. I don't know why no one wants it.

I saw Jan yesterday. I stopped in at the office. I could picture you sitting there in your big blue Geri-chair. She has your picture up on the bulletin board behind her, looking down on her desk. I hope she remembers for a long time. I know you trusted her. I'm glad she was there for you.

I wish you were here. I wish you were dozing in your armchair, your little hands splayed on the arms of it. I'd say, "Think you should go to bed, honey?" You'd nod and I'd bring you the little cup for your teeth, and your pills and inhalers and get you all ready for bed.

I don't know how I can go on without you.

***

Today is May 29. It's a Tuesday. I don't know when I last spoke to you. In any case, the weekend was crappy. It was awful weather and I was so lonely for you. I didn't get to the cemetery all last week because of the rain. It wasn't just drizzling; it was pouring, and I knew I'd get soaked and I don't like to just sit in the car. So all in all, Mom, it was a pretty awful few days and I'm feeling alone in the universe.

I talk to you all the time. I can almost guess what your answers would be to things. I can almost hear you speaking to me.

I pray every night that you'll come and bring me home. I don't belong here, Mommy. I don't fit with anyone. Like the character in the play, I have to depend on the kindness of strangers. I don't have a family anymore. We were a family, you and I. We were two, as you said, and when you're one of two, it's very different from being one. And now I'm one.

I saw Roz, the aide, today. She gave me a big hug and told me I looked good, but I don't think I do. I've never felt worse in my life. It's funny, you know? I guess they can't see that I'm like that guy in *The Wizard of Oz.* I don't have a heart anymore. It's buried with you at St. Michael's.

I don't want you to worry about me. I don't want to spoil this for you the way I spoiled so many things.

I don't think I have it in me to love anyone again. I've always made such bad choices. I don't want my heart broken again.

***

Today is Friday, it's June 1 and the beginning of a new month. May was pretty cold and you would have been a little disappointed about that.

Annie is doing a Relay for Life. People walk in teams and raise money to fight cancer. She's in Greenfield at a race track and as part of the program for this, they sold luminaries. I contributed $5 and I was able to write something for them to staple, or tape, onto the bag. I wrote "Lucia, you were the light of my life. Rest in peace. Your daughter, Pam."

Annie just called to tell me that there are about 4,000 luminaries there—all lined up around the bleachers and around the track, double rows of them. She looked and looked and in the middle of the race track, there's an arrangement of about 200 luminaries in the form of a *star*—and yours is one of those. As Annie said, "Lucy pulled that one off for you. She wanted everything she had coming to her." We laughed and I know you'd be laughing as well. Her reference was to a time you were in the hospital and the chaplain asked if you wanted to receive Communion. You nodded and said, "I want everything I've got coming."

***

Hi, Lucy. Today is Saturday, June 2, 2001. It's been raining all day. I've been working on a project. It's very boring and tedious. I wish you were here to say, "How are you doing, honey?"

I'll never see you again except in my mind. I watched the day begin and now I'm going to watch the day end, alone.

I buried a statue of St. Joseph next to the real estate sign and now I have to say a prayer every morning for nine days. It says that this has never failed and to be sure you want what you ask for. I'm asking that God will help me to sell the house soon and that it will be for a decent price and that it goes smoothly.

***

Hi, Mom, today is June 4, 2001. It's a Monday. I sold your wheelchair today. I sold it for $30 to a man who said his father is 73 and has had bypasses. Maybe he can get out a little bit more, as you were able to. It was hard to let it go. It was such a nice little wheelchair. It made it possible to do some things that we wouldn't have been able to do otherwise, such as go to funerals and out to eat. I said to Jay, "I hate to let it go. It reminds me of my mother." He said, "You have happier reminders of your mother."

The more things I get rid of that were yours, the more real it becomes to me that you're gone.

I saw Father Jim today. He told me that I'm just existing; that I dishonor you by wanting to die, by giving up. He said I can do two things for you. I can celebrate you and I can live my life with joy. He's a good man and a good priest.

Your niece called tonight. She said she wanted to put a geranium on your grave, but couldn't find the grave. I appreciated that when you died, she and her husband sent flowers and came to the wake, the funeral and the cemetery. They showed respect.

So I guess that's all I wanted to tell you: that there are a few people here who loved you and who remember, besides me.

I am happy that you're at peace, that it's not hard to breathe anymore. I'm trying hard. It's just that with such a big love, there's got to be a big grief.

***

Hi, Mommy. It's June 10. It's a Sunday. I haven't talked to you in a couple of days. I didn't get to the cemetery today. I went to church and Father Jim and his friends concelebrated a Mass in memory of his mother, who's been gone a year. He said when people we love are lost, we grieve for them always, that the grief never really goes away but that we know in our hearts that they're enjoying the promise of God. That made me cry. I felt so ill at one point that I almost passed out. It was just emotionally wrenching, you know.

Then I went down to see Gloria and Evie and had dinner with them. We looked at some pictures of the house and of you and me. I know that my life is slipping away from me and I know that I'm not living it very well. But I'm just so broken, Mom. You gave me so much. I should at least keep trying. You would have kept trying, always.

***

Hi, Mommy. Today is June 11. It's a Monday and it's been kind of a hard day for me. The Realtor and I decided to drop the listing price of the house. She said it's not the house; it's the area. It's still heartbreaking because you sacrificed so much for so many years and tried so hard to leave me with this big nest egg. The nursing home got forty grand and now we've knocked ten grand off the house.

***

Good morning, Mommy. It's June 14. It's a Thursday. I want to talk about you and nobody will listen. They tell me they'll listen and they listen for a minute and a half and then they get bored. I have so many regrets and I want someone to understand. But they just tell me that you're fine now. "She forgives you." they say, but I can't forgive myself.

I don't know why it had to be so hard for us. I look back and see how truly crazed I was at times. My God, life was hard on me: all the people I loved who didn't love me, the people I trusted who betrayed me, the people who took advantage of me and left me by the wayside with only you to pick me up and dust me off and keep me going. I know I was overwrought all the time and either terribly depressed or terribly angry. You bore the brunt of both.

It's not that we didn't have good times, because we did. We went to Cape Cod, Washington, D.C., Amish Country, New Hampshire and Vermont. We saw plays and concerts. We loved movies. We enjoyed Brownie, the best dog we could have had, and our cats and our home.

But there were more bad times, I think, than most mothers have to put up with from their children. I was with you all the time, as you used to say, so when one of us was hurting, the other knew and was sucked into that vortex. I bore your pain and my own, and you bore your pain and mine. Yet we somehow managed to make it through all the bad times.

I remember yelling at you, spewing out all my rage about you letting Bob come into the house, and seeing the hurt in your face. I'm so sorry. It wasn't your fault. No matter what the women's magazines say, how could you have known? I told you toward the end of your life that you were a wonderful mother. I hope you heard me.

I remember maybe a year or so before you died I said, "Do you forgive me, Mommy?" And you said, "Mothers forgive everything." I wonder if after that point I hurt you too much, putting you in the hospital when you didn't want to go, putting you in the nursing home when you didn't want to go, leaving you there when you didn't want to stay. "I want to go home, honey," you'd say to me. Oh God, I wanted so much to bring you home. But how could I have done it?

There were times we *were* home and you'd say, "I want to go home." I'd tell you, "This is your home." "No, no. I want to go home," you'd say. So what could I do? But I hope you forgive me now. I can't forgive myself. I hope in those last seven months I gave you enough love. I would have carried you around on a velvet cushion if it would have helped.

***

Today is June 15. It's a Friday. We had a house showing at 9:30 and they opened all the blinds so I know that they were here. I'm so hoping I'll get an offer because I really need to go, Mom. It's just too much.

I saw my former therapist. She said that having guilt and regrets and asking for forgiveness and saying how sorry I am is really a cheap out; that if I really wanted to make amends, then instead of taking on these penances, which really aren't that hard for me because I'm used to denial, what I need to do is be willing to rise to the level of your optimism, to try to be more like you. She said the best way to honor you is, if not to find happiness, to find a way to make peace with things. That seems to be the consensus.

***

Good morning, Mommy. Today is Sunday, June 17, 2001. It's about 9 a.m. It's pouring rain. Gloria and Evie have left for Maine. They said they would come to the memorial service at the nursing home. It's for all the people who died there in the past year.

I've had a very hard time these past couple of days. I'm very angry and bitter and depressed, and I'm mad at everybody who didn't love you and everybody who doesn't miss you. I particularly despise your family members.

I miss you because it's Sunday and that was our favorite day together because nothing interfered; we had the whole day. I don't miss the few months just before you went to the nursing home. Those were hard for both of us because you were so sick, although I would be happy to see you walking across the floor with your walker. I would be more gracious about caring for you. I think I could do it better now but I won't get that chance.

***

Hi, Mom. Today is June 19. It's a Tuesday. Somebody is coming to look at the house at 7. I'm hoping this will be the one. Meanwhile, I've been sick for a couple of days. I got sick Sunday afternoon and felt pretty bad yesterday but I feel a little stronger today.

It's so hard to make a life without you. You made such a pretty home. I keep up with the dishes and the bathrooms. I try to vacuum. The floors are deplorable, your word—deplorable, so there's not much I can do about them. If the house doesn't sell by August 1 and I decide to stay, that's the second thing I'll do.

The first thing is the garage roof. The third thing is the front walk and maybe the steps as well. I might have a couple of trees taken down, the gutters replaced or fixed. Of course I'd put in an alarm, all around the first floor. I don't thing I'd bother with the second.

Annie has to have surgery on her toe in September. It's going to be painful, and difficult for her to be confined to a chair or a bed for three days. If she does get that new job, it will be hard for her. I would want to be there to drive her to and from work and stuff. But if I'm living in Granby, that's not going to be easy.

Ah, maybe the best thing would be if I stayed here, you know. I could say to Evie and Gloria. "Look, I'm going to give you a month's rent for your trouble and you go ahead and rent it."

I hope you'll show me the way.

***

Today is June 21. It's 9 p.m. I went to the memorial service at the nursing home tonight. It was almost harder than your funeral because I was so numb at your funeral that I was able to get through it. They had the Lay Choir from the Dominican Monastery sing. Gloria went with me. I appreciated her driving all the way up here to do that with me. I would have been alone otherwise.

It was a small turnout but the service was nice. They sang some songs and did a couple of readings. They put up a three-sided board with pictures of the people who have died. They had the picture of you in your green shirt and brown pants holding a gerbil or some kind of little animal. But in a prominent place was the picture of you and Jan together. I said to her, "Are you going to get that picture back?" And she said, "That picture is going back on my wall."

When they called your name, I stood up and they gave me a white carnation in memory of you. They gave one to Gloria, too. She gave me hers. So I have two white carnations in the bouquet near your pictures. Doris, the lady who was your roommate at the end, the lady in the wheelchair (you used to say you envied her because she had a little car) gave me a hug and said, "I miss your mother so much. I think of her all the time. I talk about her all the time."

It was hard but I was glad to be there. It was a special place to me.

Today's the longest day of the year. Tomorrow will be a little shorter. I don't know that I'll miss you any less.

***

Today is Monday June 25. I had kind of a hard day today. I seem unable to pull it together or make anything out of my life.

I'm so afraid that as I get older I'll forget it all. It doesn't seem right that we should be apart. We were together for 55 years, and now it's been eight months that you've been dead and you're going to be dead forever.

***

Hi, Mommy, today is Tuesday, June 26, 2001. I went to the gynecologist today—not James, the one you knew, but his son. He's very nice. He said there was a note in my chart that I had been caring for my mother. I told him that you had passed away. Then I got choked up and couldn't talk. He told me that if I was still depressed in the fall, I should talk to my internist about taking medication.

I missed you being with me and going out to lunch together afterward. I missed having you to talk to. We always enjoyed each other so much.

I had a showing of the house today. It was a young couple. I left the house, as ordered, but I saw them in the driveway when I drove by later. I wish they'd make an offer. They looked like the kind of couple who would fix it up and take care of it,

I went to the cemetery and put two gerbera daisies on your stone, one red and one white. You told me once that you hoped I would visit your grave. I don't care about all the people who tell me you're not there.

Sometimes I lie on my bed and say, "The Lord giveth and the Lord taketh away." And then I cry.

***

It's June 29, a Friday. I agreed to accept the offer on the house. It's not what I had hoped for but the buyer really loves it. According to the Realtor, she loves the downstairs and the size of the kitchen and the floor plan upstairs. I think you'd be happy that somebody is coming who will love your house.

Supposedly, we're going to close about the middle of August and I'll be moving to Granby, Connecticut, to live next to Gloria and Evie in their little apartment. I don't know how long I'll stay there and I'm not even sure I'm doing the right thing.

I wish that you had had a daughter who was more fun and liked to do all the things you liked to do. I'm sorry for so many things. I'm sorry to be leaving the house that you left for me. I don't know what else to do.

***

Hi, Mommy, it's about 11:30 on July 1. It's a whole new month to live without you. I went down to see Gloria and Evie but they didn't feel good, so I felt like I was intruding, although they invited me. I hope I don't feel that way when I live there.

I got locked out last night, and got real scared and upset. It felt like a lesson that I should go. When I woke up this morning, I realized that in 45 days I won't be waking up in our house anymore. I won't be touching the things that you touched and seeing the things that you saw—not the view out the window or our pine trees getting taller.

I found myself tonight reciting your Social Security number because no one will ever ask for it again. I can't believe that we'll never laugh at each other's jokes or agree on how delicious or how pretty something is. I hope giving up the house isn't a mistake.

The poet Sara Teasdale wrote: "There will be stars forever over this place, though the house we loved and the street we loved are lost."

I think in the end we lose everything that matters to us. Everything.

***

Today is July 3. It's a Tuesday. The people who want to buy the house came and looked at it again tonight. She's a skinny little girl. She looks about 12 and her boyfriend looks about 14. But they seem to like it and to have big dreams for it. I hope they make it beautiful.

You had it pretty. I made it utilitarian. I had all the paneling done, and tried to simplify everything so it wouldn't be so much work. But when you were young and strong you poured all your love and energy and creativity into it. I marvel at you and what you were able to do with so little money.

There's an actress named Gwyneth Paltrow. (We saw her mother, Blythe Danner, once at the Williamstown Theatre Festival.) She said that her parents told her that whatever life sends your way, you should handle it with grace and nobility. You handled your life—and your death—that way.

I laid a pink carnation on your gravestone. I have the other 11 in a vase in front of your picture.

***

Hi, Mommy. Today is July 5. It's a Thursday. I've been listening to fireworks in the distance and remembering the times we saw them from our house—before all those trees grew up. Once, we went up to the attic. Another time we stood in my room. There was a time when Gloria and you and I went to Our Lady of Hope and a time when we went to the Springfield Plaza and parked facing Szot Park. I'm glad that we saw a few fireworks together. Not nearly enough. But we did see some.

The holidays are hard. We never had holidays like other people because we were alone, but who cared? We had out holidays our way. Yesterday morning I would have made French toast, and later we would have had hot dogs and potato salad, some watermelon and some ice-cream. When you were younger and well, we would have gotten in the car, taken a little ride somewhere. It would have been enough.

Being with you always was enough for me. I don't know that it was enough for you. You came from a big family. I think sometimes you missed that, but I only had you and I was pretty content to be with you.

Annie and I went down to Granby today and we painted the first floor of the apartment. It needs another coat. The cabinets have to be done. The upstairs has to be done, the bathroom. There's still an awful lot of work to do there.

Truth is I'm hoping that the deal falls through. I think this is a mistake but I lack the moral courage to cancel this deal. I'll go forward with it and try to make the best of it. I got caught up in something that I can't stop.

I miss having tea with you – Shall we have some tea? That's what you'd say, and that meant that you would like some. You made it for the first 50 years and I made it for the last five.

I just want to grab a clock hands and turn back time so you're sitting in your chair, drinking your tea, and I'm sitting in my chair drinking mine. It was enough and now nothing is enough because the thing I want is beyond reach.

I have a mammogram tomorrow. I'm terrified they will find something and terrified they won't. So you can see how screwed up I am—afraid to live, afraid to die.

I'll go to the cemetery tomorrow and I'll bring you a flower and tell you how much I love you, in case I haven't told you enough.

***

Today is July 8, I believe. It's a Sunday. I went down to see Gloria and Evie and we went to Home Depot. I bought some knobs for the cabinets and some molding for the shelf I'm going to put your bottles on. Yesterday Annie and I spent the whole day looking for blue switch plates. I'm putting a lot of attention into these little details because the apartment is so small and there's so little I can do with it.

They've begun priming the cabinets. Pretty soon everything will be white and it will be very clean and bright. My heartache is that you will never see it, although Annie believes you will. I'm going to have a pink shower curtain. I was going to go with yellow in honor of our bathroom, but I don't know if I can.

I hope to have a tag sale on Saturday and get rid of a lot of things. This is the hardest thing that I've had to do since you died. It doesn't get easier, it gets harder.

I wish you could have lived to be 95 or 96 like some people do, but I guess I was lucky to have you until you were 84. You could have been dead when you were 50-something if the stupid doctor had been right.

I know that in 40 days this will be somebody else's home and that breaks my heart in more ways than anyone could ever know.

I still find myself smiling when I picture myself at the end of my life, walking through that tunnel and seeing your bright and shining face. "Pam! Over here, honey. There you are. You came."

Today is Wednesday, July 11. I got a nice note today from a lady I met at a grief retreat. She said, "You must have had a great time with your mom." Well, yes I did. I had the best time with my mom, and now no matter how good a time I have, it pales.

Patrick was out mowing the lawn for his parents. I went over and exchanged some pleasantries, and he said, "I wrote you a note but I never sent it. You know, your mother, when I used to mow the lawn, would always give me a Coke or a ginger ale. So I said to somebody, when we meet in heaven, Lucy will have a Coke or a ginger ale ready for me." That really touched me. First, that he remembered, and secondly, that you're somebody he'd like to see in heaven.

Then he said, "You know one day she was so happy—I never saw anybody so happy, she must have talked to me for 45 minutes. She had just gotten a letter or a phone call or something and you had told her you were coming home." I don't remember when that might have been -- but you had to tell somebody so you told Pat, who was probably a teenager. What an impression it must have made on him that all these years later he remembered how happy you were that I was coming home. I wanted you to know that he smiles when he thinks of you and remembers that you used to give him a soda. I never even knew that.

***

Hi, Mom. Today is July 16. It's a Monday. I had a busy weekend. We had a tag sale on Saturday. Got rid of a lot of things. Not as many hurt this time. Then we were so tired, I couldn't do anything else. I had a project and had to work all of Sunday and a little bit this morning. I had to take a break and go visit your grave. It's the only place where I feel calm. It's as if you reach out and calm my poor troubled heart.

The woman who bought the house wants me to fix the garage roof and the damaged siding and do a couple of other things. I basically said I would do the electrical work but nothing else. I don't know what that's going to mean in terms of the contract. There's a part of me that hopes this deal falls through so I don't have to move.

My life is one big gray flat canvas without you.

***

Today is July 19. It's a Thursday. I went to the cemetery today and talked to you for a while. Wonder why I'm still here.

Jay is coming tomorrow and I'm going to have him bring everything down from the attic. I think you would have cleared out the cellar and the attic and the porches, and then started on the rooms. So that's what I'm doing.

Annie is supposed to have a tag sale on the 27th at her mother's and I'm going to bring as much as I can and try to get rid of it there.

***

Today is July 22. It's a Sunday about 8:30 in the morning, and I want to get to the cemetery before I go to church today. I'm supposed to have the junk guy come at 1. I'm desperate to get this stuff out of here. I think it will give me the feeling that I'm getting somewhere.

I've got everything out of the attic now except for the trunk and the bed. I have everything out of the cellar. The garage and my back bedroom are about 85 percent empty. So we're getting there. If the sale falls through and I have to stay, that's fine. I'll just rearrange some things. I'll use the middle room upstairs for storage.

If the sale does go through, then in a month I'll be sitting in Granby looking at the brook and wishing you were there.

It's a beautiful day. You would have liked it. The kitty is here. And we miss you.

***

Today is July 30. It's a Monday. The man from the bank is coming to appraise the house. Then about 1 o'clock, Jay is going to come and we're going to take your bed down. This is an incredibly hard thing for me. I've walked up the stairs and looked through the slats in the banister and seen the foot of that bed since I was a little girl. Taking it down is another acknowledgement that you're never coming home. My heart still doesn't understand how you can be gone forever.

***

Good morning. It's Sunday, August 5. I'm getting ready to go to Mass. I wish that I had taken you during those years when I wouldn't go. I know that would have been a comfort to you. Maybe that's why I have my anxiety attacks. Because I didn't give you that comfort, I feel that I don't deserve it.

In the shower this morning, I remembered washing your hair. How pretty it always looked when it dried. I wish that I could have kept you safe from all harm. But I don't have to do that anymore because nothing can hurt you now.

What is the Scripture quote? "Eye has not seen, nor ear heard nor has the mind of man imagined what wonders God has prepared for those who love him."

I spent last night showing Annie all your crafts, all your painting. I wanted her to know that you weren't always just a sick old woman, that you were vibrant and creative and interesting.

***

Hi, Mom, it's Monday, August 6.

I let you down that day at Woodbridge's when you fell. I should have been walking with you. I was going to get out of the car and open the door. You moved too quickly. You always wanted to get to me. We just wanted to get to each other.

***

Chapter Twelve: Moving On

It's August 9, 2001. It's a Thursday and I got word today that the buyer got her financing. The house is sold. We should close on Wednesday morning. They'll be shutting off all the utilities next week and I'll be moving to Granby. I can't believe it, Mommy, that in less that a week I'll be gone from our home.

I contracted with a couple, Ed and Helen Pelletier, to make a video of the house with some words from me on it. They brought the finished video down tonight and we watched it in the living-room, which is filled with boxes. It's beautiful. I think you'd like it a lot. It is "a tribute to Lucia Cummings and the house she made a home."

***

Well Mom, today is August 26; it's a Sunday morning. The last time I talked to you was August 9. I'm sitting in my little apartment in Granby. But it is not going to work out for me. It is too small. Why didn't I listen to my gut when I kept feeling it would be?

The move was exhausting. I had the contents of six rooms, a cellar, an attic, two porches and a garage. I moved into a two-room apartment and a couple of storage units. The transition was too much, too soon. I am overwhelmed.

Yesterday, I put a deposit down on a condo in a place called Rosewood Estates in Southwick. It is a three-room unit with a full basement. It looks very safe and very peaceful, although it may not be private enough for me.

It's funny because I think I could move every year for the rest of my life and never feel the kind of sadness that I felt when I left our home. I don't think that loss has even set in for me yet.

Yesterday, I went to the cemetery and I brought you a handful of yellow flowers. I was sitting there missing you and crying because I wished that we could be making this move together. I looked down at your stone and I said, "I hope you like your yellow flowers." I said it out loud and then I looked up and something passed right before my eyes. I have no idea if it was some kind of insect or some kind of a dandelion thing, or what, but it was white. It kind of shimmered, and it drifted past me and very slowly across your grave and over the next couple of graves and into the distance.

***

Hi, Mom. (No date given.) It's been a long time since I recorded. I don't want to do it now because it hurts so much. I also find that it's painful to look at some of your pictures. I'm suffering for the lack of you. It's so hard to be without you. I have some nice evenings, you know. I watch a movie with Gloria and Evie but then I want to get in my car and go *home*. I go to the cemetery and hope to get that feeling of closeness to you. But I don't feel it lately.

The only thing that keeps me putting one foot in front of the other is the hope that you're somewhere where I will see you again. If there is some way you can give me a sign, I'd be grateful.

***

It's Thursday, September 6, 2001. I'm sitting here in the apartment at Gloria and Evie's place. I want to pick up the phone and call you and say, "I'll be home in a little while. I'll stop and get some cranberry juice."

I look over at your picture and you're smiling at me. I feel like you're right here. You wrote a poem once and said that the world is made for people who come two by two and that when you're one, everything is bleak and empty. You were so right.

I am moving closer to the purchase of the condo in Southwick. We're supposed to close on the 24th or the 26th of October. The sooner the better, as far as I'm concerned. I know that the first few days I'm there I'm going to feel like I don't fit. But I think it's the best thing.

So hold me in your heart, Mom. I always think of that song that Connie Francis sang, "Mama." I think it ends, "You will live in my memory, until the day when we're together again." Goodnight.

Chapter Thirteen: Now and Beyond

It is now 2010. I stopped recording the journal years ago. But I still speak to you all the time. I hope you hear and that you are near. If so, you know what I am about to tell you. But I will recount it here for the sake of completing this account.

I lived in Southwick for almost 18 months. During that time, I had a bad accident on black ice and totaled my car. My friends drove me home from the hospital and helped me into my condo. "Call if you need anything," they said when they left. I remember thinking, "Need anything? I need everything."

I was on crutches and my legs ached from my having jammed my feet against the floorboard when I crashed into the car in front of me. I ate peanut butter out of the jar: I couldn't manage anything else at first.

I remained on crutches for weeks. It was a cold and snowy February and it was hard to get my mail and my groceries. The supermarket was 5 miles from my door. I realized that the country is fine for families, but I needed to live in a city, where I would have access to stores and public transportation.

I sold the condo and left Southwick in May 2003. I rented a four-room apartment near my alma mater, a mile or two from our house. So I live in a neighborhood that abuts ours.

After you died, I never went back to full-time work. Fortunately, I had learned frugality from you. I took my retirement income as soon as I could and I still do editing at home—for a client I like and respect. She sends me a bonus at Christmas. It makes me feel valued.

A lot has happened in the years you have been gone. I have had another surgery, nothing major. I have been diagnosed with diabetes and struggle to manage it. I have lost Kitty and, for the first time in my life, I do not have a pet.

Our dear friend Ruth has Alzheimer's—diagnosed when she was in her 50s. How ironic that she was the one who sat with you every Saturday so I could get out. She is in a residence now and her husband is alone. Annie has been with a nice man for several years; I am happy for her, but I miss the time she used to give me. Gloria and I talk every day. She is the only person I know who really remembers you when you were full of life.

Some friends have fallen away over the years. I have made a couple of others. Christie and I have dinner once a week. Father Jim has been a blessing; he is still in my life although I have left the Church again. I cannot look at the world as it is and wrap my mind or heart around the notion of a loving God who is engaged in our lives. I am trying to find another way of believing, another path to peace.

I fear the future – especially the prospect of blindness, because of the diabetes, and dependency. I fear the loss of the few people I love.

I meant to stay in this little apartment for a year and then buy another condo. But the year became two, then five, now seven. There is a little restaurant nearby. I can walk to the library -- I have begun to read again, as you would have urged me to do.

It is not much, but it is almost enough. I try not to wish for more, hoping to spare myself more disappointment. But sometimes, against my better judgment, against my will, there is a small flare of hope.

I remember one time many years ago, before you died, I was talking to Sally. She is a healer and a gentle soul. I was going on about you and I said something like, "You must think it's odd that at this age I am so attached to my mother." She was quiet for a while. Then she said, "I think most people have to leave home to find their soul mates."

I think of you all the time, Mom, in good moments and bad. As some had predicted, my memories seem to center on the years when you were healthy and vital. One in particular comes to me quite often. We were at a mall in Chicopee one day. You were probably in your 60s. We were sitting in an area that had benches, with people walking by in both directions.

A little boy, about 5, holding a balloon, was walking with his mother, and maybe his grandmother, and they were approaching the place where we sat. Going in the opposite direction was a loud group of teenaged boys. As they passed the child, one of them snagged the balloon and kept walking. His pals thought it was hilarious.

You got up and followed the teens and when you caught up to the one with the balloon, you reached for it and said cheerfully, "Give the baby back his balloon, fella." He looked stunned but did not resist. You returned the balloon to the little boy, then came back and sat down with a little smile on your face.

I don't know who else would have had the courage to confront those boys. I'm sure you were intimidated by them. Yet you did it—because you could not bear to see the look of sorrow on that child's face. You had the power to make things right and so you did.

That is who you were. That is why I still grieve.

The End

About the Author

Pam Robbins has a master's degree in Language and Literature and worked as a journalist for thirty years. She lived most of her life in Springfield, Massachusetts, and now resides in neighboring Chicopee.

www.ingramcontent.com/pod-product-compliance
Ingram Content Group UK Ltd.
Pitfield, Milton Keynes, MK11 3LW, UK
UKHW020241250726
13967UKWH00001B/486